How to Produce a Small Newspaper

How to Produce a Small Newspaper

by the Editors of the Harvard Post

Second Edition

THE HARVARD COMMON PRESS

HARVARD AND BOSTON, MASSACHUSETTS

The Harvard Common Press
535 Albany Street
Boston, Massachusetts 02118

Printed in the United States of America.

Library of Congress Cataloging in Publication Data

Main entry under title:
How to produce a small newspaper.

  Bibliography: p.
  Includes index.
  1. Newspaper publishing. 2. Community newspapers.
I. Harvard Post.
PN4734.H67 1983   338.4'7070572   83-12579
ISBN 0-916782-40-9
ISBN 0-916782-39-5 (pbk.)

Line drawings by Martha Dillard
Cover design by Peter Good

10 9 8 7 6 5 4 3 2

*To the memory of
Leon Delaney,
who got us started,*

*and to all the Inklings
who keep us going.*

Introduction

THE TRADITIONAL PORTRAIT of a small, weekly newspaper depicts the editors—often husband and wife—sitting in their cramped Main Street office piled high with old newspapers, hard at work pounding out news stories and editorials, calling local merchants for advertisements, then running out to the backshop to set type in preparation for that week's edition. Life on a small newspaper has always been hectic, and it will undoubtedly remain so. The editors (who are often the publishers as well) must be masters of all the skills—selling ads, reporting the news, writing editorials, setting type, preparing the paper for print—that go into the production of a successful small paper.

Traditionally, publishing a small newspaper has been an expensive proposition as well. Besides paying for a shop and a staff, the publisher usually had to invest a substantial amount of money in printing equipment —a Linotype machine on which to set type in the form of metal slugs or "lines" of type, and a large printing press. To make that equipment pay its way, the newspaper publisher in the past often had to take on job printing— stationery, wedding invitations, posters, billheads, and the like.

Those days are over. The technology of printing and typesetting has come so far in recent decades that it is now possible to start a small publication with almost no initial investment. A small newspaper of the highest quality can be produced economically, these days, in a small office or in a corner of your own home. You need one major piece of equipment, a typesetting machine—which is nevertheless compact, can be rented rather than purchased, and requires only good typing skills to operate. A printing press is no longer necessary, or even desirable, as part of the equipment you should own if you plan to publish your own paper. All this has come from the refinement of offset printing; it has eliminated the use of cumbersome metal type, simplified the reproduction of photographs and other forms of nontype illustrations, and generally reduced the amount of time needed to produce a small publication.

The computer age has brought many changes in the newspaper business; indeed, many large newspapers feel that their existence is seriously threatened by the advent of news data banks, video publications, and burgeoning television coverage. To the small newspaper, though, computers represent only progress; they can facilitate typesetting, recordkeeping, and accounting, and it is extremely unlikely that they will ever replace the small newspaper in disseminating the news. No matter how extensive the data bases of the future may become, we are willing to bet that your neighbors will not sit down to consult them on Friday evening to find out whose baby was born that week or what the selectmen have decided to do about the weed problem in the town pond. There will always be a need for good newspapers on the local level; and those in the small newspaper profession universally agree that readers are extraordinarily loyal to such publications. Because of this, the weekly newspaper can be a very stable and rewarding business.

Throughout this book we use the term "small newspaper"; and perhaps at the start we should tell you something about our own. The *Harvard Post*, the weekly newspaper that we publish, was started by two of us in 1973 in a small Massachusetts town. Flying in the face of conventional journalistic wisdom, we decided at the outset to concentrate on the news and concerns of just one town—and to produce a newspaper that was of the highest quality, in both its graphics and its writing.

Ours is a small-format or tabloid-size paper—that is, it has a page size of 11½ inches by 16½ inches—and we usually produce editions of 16, 20, or 24 pages, depending on how much advertising and editorial matter we have. Our circulation is about 2,000, a figure which means that virtually every household in our community pays for and receives a copy of the *Post* each week.

The techniques and ideas discussed in this book can be of use in the production of many different types of small publications—newsletters or magazines, for example. But what we are primarily describing here is how to produce an offset-printed, small-format newspaper, probably one with a relatively small circulation that comes out on a weekly, biweekly, or monthly schedule. We think that the tabloid format makes sense for a small newspaper. It is easier to design and paste up; it is more pleasant to handle, look at, and read; and it is in most ways more economical to produce. Even some established and reputable daily newspapers, like the Christian Science Monitor, have in recent years gone from full-size or "metro" format to the more compact tabloid.

This book is mainly concerned with the mechanics of newspaper production; we have assumed that the reader already possesses a love for good newspapers and wants to know how he can make one himself. The intellectual and aesthetic rewards of succeeding at such an enterprise should be obvious. We feel obliged to point out, however, that publishing a small newspaper has certain disadvantages. The hours are long, for one thing, and the pay can be lousy. All too often, despite the best-laid plans, our weekly production marathon ends in an exhausted frenzy, from which we have barely recovered before work on the next week's edition must begin. Our newspaper supports itself, certainly, and contributes to the support of a number of people, but it will never make us or anyone else rich.

The richness of the newspaper life is of a different sort. There is no better way that we know of to become intimately involved in a community of people than to be a newspaper editor. Ultimately, we believe in small newspapers because we believe in small communities and in the value of their social and political institutions.

A small newspaper's community need not be a geographical one; its circulation might comprise a widely scattered readership linked by a common interest of any nature. Some of the finest small newspapers in the country today serve such special interest groups; and whether their purpose is political, environmental, or cultural, they bring together people and ideas at least as powerfully as a more locally focused publication. Whatever its readership, and whatever its viewpoint, each new publication adds to our collective independence by resisting the appalling homogenization of culture and information brought on by a centralized news establishment.

There is probably no better description of the need in a democratic society for small newspapers—and many of them—than these words penned in 1940 by Henry Beetle Hough in *Country Editor:*

> Most writers predict that in years to come there will be fewer and fewer newspapers. They do this because of what has happened in the past, and it is always easier to predict something which has already happened. But my prophecy is that there will be more newspapers in the future. Because the manufacturers of machinery and equipment, already facing a restricted market, will see that the genius of the machine age at last gets down to small publishing units so that they may buy and use tools

adapted to their own needs. Because the formula of mass circulation and mass advertising is self-limiting and there are many signs that the point of diminishing returns is being reached and passed. Because an improving social conscience and broader intelligence will hardly let the preservation of great circulations count against changes which are in the interest of human betterment—including, it may well be, government help for consumers who are now exploited. Because there is not room enough in journalism today for men and women who should be able to claim newspaper careers, and the reason there is not room enough is artificial and without real validity from a social standpoint. After all, it is right that millions of bricks should be alike, but not that millions of newspapers should be alike.

In the ferment around us we see one thing which is more hopeful than the others, a striving toward greater dignity for the individual and his spirit, and is not this striving—the onward reach of democracy—a sufficiently valid reason to work with the rest for a decentralization of the press?

We have added two new chapters to this second edition—on the structure of a small newspaper's staff and on editing—and, in addition, the chapters on typography and financial matters have been substantially revised to reflect changes in the industry and to include some of the new things we have learned in the six years since this book first appeared. We are indebted to the many readers of the first edition who have written to us and sent us copies of their own small publications, and we welcome comments, criticism, and commiseration on the present volume.

Kathleen Cushman, Ed Miller, and Larry Anderson
Harvard, Massachusetts
May 1983

Contents

How to
Produce a
Small
Newspaper

1 The Newspaper Staff

IF YOU ARE CONSIDERING STARTING A SMALL NEWSPAPER one of the first things you will have to decide is who will carry out the work of producing it. Planning and managing the newspaper's operation, writing and editing its contents, selling its ads, keeping its books, setting its type, and laying it out for the printer may all be within your capability at the start—indeed, for the first few years of the Harvard Post we managed to scrape by with help from only a few generous contributors. But eventually we learned what is perhaps the most important lesson for any small newspaper: that the involvement of other people in a publication is the surest means towards its success. When you can expand your staff to include people in the community who contribute their talents to your publication— even if you can afford to pay them very little—their participation will generate an interest and spirit that will soon show its results in higher circulation. More than that, such helpers will sustain you through the difficult decisions and grueling work of editing and publishing a newspaper; their camaraderie will lighten the latest hours; and when you must be absent for some unforeseen reason their experience in carrying out crucial tasks will prove invaluable.

Although your budget will probably be spartan, we think it is essential that every contributor be paid. No matter how small, a paycheck says to each reporter, photographer, and columnist that you place a real value on his or her work. The fact that you are willing to share the financial rewards of publishing your newspaper, however meager, with your contributors assures them that their own sacrifices in working for you are meaningful; and the recognition they will get from readers will make up to some extent for how little they are paid.

It is all too easy, in the hectic rush towards the weekly deadline, to lose sight of the importance of your staff. You, after all, will probably bear the brunt of the exhausting schedule; and it is on your shoulders that final responsibility rests. But your attitude towards each person who helps you will affect your operations more than you might imagine possible. For each contributor, her or his part in the newspaper is of vital importance and interest—whether it involves shooting and printing a photograph, covering a meeting, or selling an ad. If you neglect to acknowledge this by a sensitive and appreciative response, you will soon find yourself resented and eventually abandoned. Even in the throes of production day, it is worth calling that photographer to ask if he minds your drastic cropping of the picture he submitted, or consulting with the advertising manager on the placement of a troublesome ad. Such actions will repay themselves a hundredfold in the loyalty and forbearance of your staff.

Some of the jobs on your newspaper you will want to take on yourself; others you will look for other people to fulfill. In any case, you should understand each function well enough to be able to carry it out in an emergency. Not only will this help you hire the best people for each job, but it will give you a firsthand appreciation of the trials each staffer must undergo. Here are descriptions of the jobs that must be done on any small newspaper. Look through them carefully before you decide to do it all yourself.

Publisher. If you are beginning your own small newspaper, or even if you are buying one that is already established, chances are that you will have the title of publisher yourself. In general on small newspapers, the owner is also the publisher, although when a paper is owned by a group of partners, for example, one person is usually designated to hold this position.

The publisher is the chief administrator of the newspaper. He or she is responsible for seeing that all the functions of the paper are carried out efficiently; that its financial affairs are in order; and that its staff is complete and of the best available quality. It's usually the publisher who negotiates the contract with the printer and the lease with the landlord, decides what kind of equipment the paper needs and can afford, and sets the advertising and subscription rates. The publisher decides who the editor of the paper will be, and also hires other key staff members, though he or she need not be involved, for example, in screening reporters or other contributors. Most often, the publisher of a small newspaper also carries out one other top role, usually that of editor or advertising manager. If you are beginning a small husband-and-wife operation, as we did with the Harvard Post, there is nothing wrong with both of you sharing the title of publisher.

Ultimately, the publisher bears legal responsibility for the content of the newspaper. If someone sues the paper for libel or some other wrong, the publisher will be a defendant.

Is it proper for a publisher who is not also serving as editor to interfere in editorial decisions? Strictly speaking, no. In the ideal newspaper office the sole editorial control that the publisher wields is the power to replace an editor who makes bad decisions. But in the real world there are few publishers who can resist the temptation to be backseat editors. The smart editor consults the publisher when tough questions arise. The wise publisher gives his advice and then says, "You're the editor. You decide." Oddly, this little scene can take place even when publisher and editor are the same person.

Editor. The editor decides on everything that goes into the newspaper—news, features, photographs and artwork—and sees that it is of the highest possible quality. He or she keeps track of community events, assigns stories to reporters, assembles the material to be included in each issue, and goes over it carefully for accuracy, objectivity, thoroughness, and style. Very often the editor will write a good deal of material as well; in any case, she will write the editorials expressing the official opinions of the newspaper. The editor is also responsible for the placement of stories in the paper; even if she does not end up laying out each edition, she will supervise the people who do, and her decisions will determine what emphasis is given to each story. The editor usually writes the headlines.

We have found that the difficult job of editor is best shared by two people. The support of a co-editor can give one courage to pursue an unpopular course; the restraint of a co-editor can prevent disastrous errors of judgment. Even the editor must undergo editing of any material he or she writes, and this is best carried out by a respected and experienced co-editor. Sharing the task of editor greatly reduces the panic and stress of coming down with the flu or taking an occasional vacation. And it means that when an aggrieved reader calls up with a complaint, you will have a sympathetic and helpful sounding board after you hang up the phone.

At the Harvard Post we give additional support to the editors by naming one or two people as *associate editors*. This is often a welcome promotion for an experienced reporter who would like to take more part in the newspaper's production and its editorial decisions. Our associate editors share in most of the editor's tasks—suggesting stories, editing copy, drafting editorials, doing layout—but they do not have final authority over what goes into the paper. The position of associate or assistant editor is an excellent training ground for future editors.

Reporters. If you intend to cover the news of your community, you will need to have on your staff at least two reporters. Largely, the task of the reporter on a small newspaper is to attend official meetings and to write up the news that emerges from them in a clear and objective way. (More on this is included in *Content,* Chapter 2.)

No matter how much energy the editor has, he or she will not be able to cover all the news alone; there will always be schedule conflicts between various boards and groups. The best solution is to recruit and develop a few good writers, spend some time with them explaining the background information they will need to know, and assign each a "beat"—that is, a particular group or issue, such as the school board or police and court news.

Reporters should be encouraged to go beyond simply reporting what happens at public meetings; assign news features and background pieces that will keep important issues and events in the paper even when no meeting has occurred. A dependable stable of reporters who contribute something to every edition is an invaluable asset to the small newspaper staff.

Other contributors. Those people who can supply you every week with art, photographs, book reviews, recipe columns, opinion columns, club news, and the like are an integral part of the staff. Each contribution may be minor taken alone; but together they constitute the essential material that will fill the pages of the paper as those frightening holes appear on deadline day. In addition, as we have mentioned, each contributor widens your readership in geometric proportion, and makes your paper truly belong to the community. The editor will soon learn which contributors can be counted on to produce good material on time, and how to encourage them as well as to deal tactfully with less talented aspirants to newspaper work.

Copy editor. Not only should the material that goes into your paper be edited for content, but it should also be checked for accuracy, grammar, and style. This task is called copy editing, and is described more fully on page 31. At the Harvard Post the editors and associate editors are responsible for copy editing the news and features. We also try to hire typographers who can be trained in copy editing; they can then make minor editorial adjustments as they set material into type.

Advertising representative. Depending on the size of your community, selling ads may be a job for one person or for several; you may find that it is best to appoint an advertising manager with several representatives working as her assistants. This is a critical job, and one which must be filled with the utmost care. We address it in detail in *Advertising,* pages 100–114.

Whoever your advertising salespeople are, it is inevitable that conflict will arise between them and the editors. This occurs in every publishing venture, no matter what its size, and you should be prepared to deal with it equably. The advertising manager will always push for more ads, more favorable placement of ads in the paper, various editorial concessions to advertisers, and extensions of deadlines. But to the editors more ads mean more layout work, more copy to write and edit, more headaches for them; and they will resent pressures to alter editorial policies or stances to suit advertisers' interests. The salesperson will argue, correctly, that without the advertisers there could be no paper at all. The editor will respond, just as correctly, that the newspaper's first responsibility is to serve the interests of its readers, not those of advertisers.

One of the publisher's responsibilities is to mediate such disputes, to ensure that both sides are treated fairly, to work towards a healthy balance between advertising volume and high editorial quality, and to encourage the advertising and editorial staff to accept their natural antagonism with good grace.

Business manager. Someone must oversee the day-to-day operations of the newspaper: pay its rent and other bills, maintain its premises, supervise or perform its endless bookkeeping tasks, keep it supplied with materials for the production process, keep its machinery in good repair, answer the telephone, and deal with customers of all sorts. This person is the business manager, or general manager, or office manager. He or she will supervise the comings and goings of the various part-time staff members, keep the office open during its appointed hours, and deal with all kinds of non-editorial problems that arise daily.

On a small publication the publisher or even an editor might take on these responsibilities; whoever it is, though, should be efficient, organized, careful, and gifted at dealing with people.

Bookkeeper. Whether or not you use the services of an accountant—and we recommend that you do—you will need someone to keep your books. This need not be a full-time employee; at the Post the bookkeeper works out of her home and is technically a consultant. The bookkeeper will take care of sending out bills and recording payments, and will keep up with subscription and advertising records. If a computer is available, the bookkeeper will enter the appropriate data in its files. More on setting up a bookkeeping system with or without a computer appears in *Financial Matters,* pages 142–155.

Typographer. In order for written copy to be made ready for the printer, it must first be set into type using whatever system of composition is available to you. This task is carried out by your typographers, or compositors. The ideal compositor is a perfectionist with a good sense of typography and a copy editor's command of English; most important, though, is that the typographer be a fast, accurate typist with a mechanical bent (so she or he will better understand the workings of the typesetting machine). Word processing experience is a big plus, and the ability to keep long, demanding hours on deadline day is an absolute necessity.

We have found that it is best to employ two typographers, so that neither must bear the burden alone; their numbers, of course, will also depend on the amount of material you must produce. Make sure, in any case, that more than one person knows enough about your typesetting equipment to be able to operate it in an emergency. (More on typesetting appears in *Typography,* Chapter 5.)

Advertising production manager. Someone must take on the task of organizing into type the material with which the advertising representatives come in every deadline day, so that the ads appear in a tasteful, attractive form and can be placed by the editors onto the layout pages. This person is the advertising production manager, though often these responsibilities are fulfilled by an editor or someone else who also does other jobs. Whoever it is should know how to specify different sizes and styles of type for the contents of each ad, so that it can go to the typographer, and should have strong layout and pasteup skills.

It is best for the ads to be completely prepared and placed on the newspaper layout sheets before the editors begin to place news copy; for this reason we have found it most effective to have a separate advertising production manager rather than calling on an editor to do such work. (There is a more detailed explanation of these tasks in *Design and Layout,* pages 74–79.)

Layout help. You will be grateful if there are people available to help paste up the paper on deadline day, to proofread it one more time, to size pictures and prepare them for the printer, and to carry out the endless, meticulous tasks of layout. Even if such people work only a couple of hours a week, they can save you hours of labor at a critical point, when the editorial staff is suffering from overload and fatigue. Specific instructions for layout and pasteup helpers are included in Chapter 7.

Office help. You may find that it is useful to have on your staff a few people who perform miscellaneous office tasks: cleaning up, answering the telephone when the editors are sleeping it off the morning after the paper goes to the printer, sticking address labels onto the copies in preparation for mailing, and so on. If you plan to maintain an orderly office with dependable office hours, people like this can be a godsend. With luck, they may develop hidden talents in the job, and graduate to other newspaper duties as well.

Legal adviser. Find someone with a thorough working knowledge of the laws in your state who is willing to act as your counselor, at least informally. The publisher and editors should study the libel and copyright laws so that they can avoid most potential problems, but from time to time a question that defies the layman's understanding will come up. Any article that suggests the possibility of a lawsuit, even after judicious editing, should be read by a lawyer before publication.

Students and interns. Do not neglect the potential of students and interns, who are often willing to work very hard for the experience a newspaper job offers. We like to take on such workers only after they have shown some evidence of being able to write well, and then assign them to cover occasional or less important meetings, or to write features that might not otherwise get done. We also train them in layout and pasteup, and involve them to the greatest degree possible in every aspect of producing the paper.

In return for this broad exposure to the small newspaper trade, they are paid little or nothing, but they end their terms with a strong resume and a realistic picture of the profession. Harvard Post interns have gone on to much more imposing jobs—one went directly to a position at United Press International—on the basis of the portfolios they assembled with us. Note: it is rarely worthwhile to take on an intern who cannot stay for at least three months, and six is preferable.

2 Content

THE CONTENT OF YOUR NEWSPAPER depends, of course, upon who you hope and expect will be reading it. And once you've settled upon the community you expect to serve—whether it's one defined by geography or by shared interests—the standard for choosing the material that goes into your paper will be its relevance and usefulness to that audience.

The primary tools you have to work with in putting together the *editorial* portion of your newspaper—that is, everything except the ads—are words, photographs, and other forms of artwork. The variety of subjects, events, and personalities you can describe with these tools is endless, no matter how small a community your paper is serving. Your primary goals should be to make the articles that you publish scrupulously accurate and of the highest stylistic quality; to make photographs and illustrations informative, entertaining, and original; and to present your articles and illustrations in a neat, attractive, and logical format.

With those guidelines in mind, it's important also to consider one other crucial factor—*how* you present information. Where in the paper to place a particular article, whether to byline it, what kind of headline to put on it—these are a few of the things you'll have to decide for every item. The decisions you make will affect how the information you are presenting is perceived by your readers.

NEWS

News is whatever happens in your community, whatever that community may consist of. Events on a smaller scale may not seem to carry the same excitement and importance as those reported in the daily papers, on television, or in national newsmagazines, but in the lives of your readers they are probably even more important. And while the people in your community can get their hands on plenty of sources of information about what's going on in the larger world, your paper may be the only objective, comprehensive source of news about what's happening close to home.

If yours is a community newspaper, thorough and accurate coverage of local events should be a top priority. Although time and staff are certain to be limited, try to arrange for reporters to cover as many of the important political meetings and events in your community as possible. Town and city councils, boards of selectmen or aldermen, school boards, planning and zoning boards, utility commissions, finance committees, tax assessors, housing and health boards—these and numerous other official municipal bodies continually consider and make decisions on matters that will have significant effects on the lives of your readers. Many of those meetings are tedious, both to attend and to report. You will make some enemies in the process of reporting on them; but your paper will certainly gain local attention, respect, and perhaps influence if it can establish a reputation for accurate, impartial, thorough, and aggressive reporting of local politics and government.

There are some unique pleasures and pitfalls related to reporting the news for a small paper. For one thing, it won't be long before you get to know just about everyone in the community. Certain people will begin to offer you inside information, "hot tips," and all sorts of gossip about things that are going on in town. Some do this just because they like you and your paper; others want to use you to promote their own point of view or grind a particular axe. It's good to encourage people who come to you with news you might not otherwise get, but don't let your newspaper become a one-sided outlet for the views and interests of any one person or group, to the exclusion of opposing opinions. It is important for the ultimate success of your paper that it not be identified with any one faction of the community; to achieve this, the editor must talk with, and be willing to listen to, people of all persuasions. This will insure that virtually every tendril on the grapevine reaches you sooner or later.

It also means that in the course of pursuing the news you're likely to step on the toes of people you know well. Henry Beetle Hough, editor of the Vineyard Gazette on the island of Martha's Vineyard, writes as follows about the power of the press in a small community:

A country editor is often considered a softish or craven member of a profession in which forthrightness and crusading zeal are, or used to be, ranked high, but anyone is foolish who reaches this judgment lightly. Whatever the country editor does, he does to an acquaintance or a friend whom he will soon be meeting on the street or in the stores or at a church supper. He'll be aware of the consequences personally and perhaps for a long time; he's not like the city newspaper editor who said to a frayed and beaten-up reporter, "You go back and tell that fellow he can't intimidate *me*."

Yet the country editor knows that the news must be printed, and generally prints it. [*Once More the Thunderer*]

Investigative reporting. It's not enough just to report the news that happens to come your way; you've got to go out and look for news. Don't be satisfied with simply sending a reporter to the town council meetings every other week. That reporter should be in contact regularly with each member of the council, and with any other people who are privy to the inner workings of the board. The most interesting news in any community rarely surfaces for the first time at public meetings—especially if the officials involved know that a reporter will be there. Even in places where open-meeting or "sunshine" laws are in effect, the people who hold political power generally find ways to keep the public in the dark where "bad news" is concerned— "bad news" being anything that reflects poorly on those in charge. The best remedy for this disease is a curious, persistent reporter who asks a lot of questions and listens carefully to the answers.

There are many sources of news other than local politics, of course. Try to keep track of what your state and federal legislators are up to—not just what they say they're up to in their press releases. Get to know them, ask them questions about their positions on issues, let them know your paper is keeping an eye on their performance.

Learn to use the telephone; it's the reporter's greatest tool. Not everyone has the nerve or the presence of mind to be able to ask a tough question of an intimidating bigwig in a face-to-face situation. But it's not nearly as hard to collect your thoughts later, figure out what you want to know, dial a number, and say, "Mayor Stanky, this is Mary Johnson of the Chronicle. What's the reasoning behind your decision . . . ."

Local items. Sports events, the activities of local clubs and organizations, court proceedings, police and fire reports—all these are possible sources of news for your paper, depending on how much time your staff has to collect such information. You might even try to develop your own group of "stringers," people who can write reasonably well and who can be depended upon to supply regular reports on a particular organization or subject.

One tradition of small-town journalism is to include the names and photographs of as many people as possible in the paper—the idea being, at least in part, that all those names and faces are potential subscribers. And the traditional way of realizing that goal is running "locals," very short news items describing the comings, goings, and doings of the townspeople. Many columns of country papers have been filled with items such as: "Mr. and Mrs. Randolph Bartholomew of Pine Hill Road returned last Monday from a two-week vacation in Ames, Iowa, where they were visiting their daughter Susan."

You may choose not to run locals; but a page or part of a page with a heading such as *People* could include many short items describing births, marriages, and people who have received awards or have new jobs, as well as many other minor occurrences that may be as important and interesting to your readers as the most dramatic local political event. Some such "news," like the names of the recently elected officers of the garden club, may seem too routine even for the "People" column; we have initiated a separate column on the same page, labeled "Clubs," and here we present items that otherwise might not make it into the paper at all.

It's worth remembering that the strength of small-scale journalism springs from its closeness to the people, places, and events about which it reports. The vitality of that tradition is worth preserving.

Press releases. Before long you'll find yourself on the mailing list of every organization in your area, and you'll soon be buried under their press releases. Some of this information will be welcome and useful, helping both to inform your readers and to fill up your paper without the expenditure of too much time or money.

But many organizations and their press agents will feel insulted if you don't print their releases—or if you don't run them exactly as they've written them. Stick to your editorial prerogative to use only those items that really deserve to go in, and to leave out anything that is unimportant or unnecessary. Many press releases are atrociously written and need considerable editing or rewriting. Especially watch out for—and don't print—press releases that are really advertisements in disguise.

We have a short guide that we give to local people who have been given the task of writing publicity for their organizations and clubs. After describing the format that we prefer and our deadline requirements, the guide makes the following remarks about style:

> Your goal should be to convey information to the reader as clearly and as quickly as possible. Put the most important things first. If you are announcing a coming event, be sure to say what it is and when and where it will be at the beginning of the article, though not necessarily all in one

sentence. If you are reporting an important piece of news about your organization, put that right at the beginning. You might start an article like this: "A community vasectomy project will be run in town next year by the Planned Parenthood Club, it was decided at the club's regular meeting last Thursday." Don't start this way: "The Planned Parenthood Club [or whatever] held a meeting last Thursday," or, even worse, "On Thursday, February 4, a meeting was held by the Planned Parenthood Club."

There should be a fairly logical progression in your article from the most important material to the least important. If you submit a five-paragraph story, keep in mind that we may have to eliminate two paragraphs to make it fit; therefore, you should put the things that you would least mind having cut out in the last two paragraphs.

The Harvard Post strives for a unity of tone in its news columns, and this principle is applied even to the shortest items and press releases. It doesn't mean that your submissions have to be uniformly dry and color-less; it simply means that we are going to apply our standards of objec-tivity and restraint to everything that appears in the Post as news. Some publicity writers aspire in their press releases to the style of a carnival sideshow barker: "Come One, Come All to the entertainment event of the year! Dance your hearts out to the rapturous sounds of the Norman Bonomo Quartet at next Saturday's Winter Whoopie Dinner-Dance sponsored by the Benevolent Order of Moles." This kind of pitch might be acceptable in an advertisement (and you are welcome to place one in the paper) but it is not acceptable in the guise of news.

Try to confine any flat statements in your article to demonstrable facts. If you want to say that the dance is going to be a great success, that *opinion* should be attributed to someone: " 'This will be the entertain-ment event of the year,' says Henry Fenster, president of the Moles." Avoid all exhortations to the reader, and look out for cliches and writing that is self-consciously cute.

Be aware of the political implications of what you write. If a partic-ular opinion or point of view is expressed in a newspaper article without being attributed to a specific person or group, readers will assume that the opinion expressed is that of the editors. If you are writing a report of a club meeting, for instance, try to quote people directly or else paraphrase their statements and add "So-and-So said," or "she said," rather than presenting those statements as if they were facts.

Long lists of names often present a problem for us. In general, we try to include such information—the names of the new officers of a club, for example—in our "People" or "Clubs" columns, and you are welcome to send us items that would fit appropriately under those categories. Please try to keep the size of the list under control by including only the more important items.

You are welcome to suggest a possible headline for your article, but don't be upset if we don't use it. Sometimes it just won't fit; or it might not be in the proper style dictated for newspaper headlines. Writing the headlines is both a chore and a privilege that is traditionally reserved for the editors.

Business news. While press releases that are little more than advertisements in disguise should be kept out of the paper, there are many events in the economic life of a community that are legitimate news. Often the same press release that is unacceptable in itself will provide a useful clue to a real story. For example, a new business in town may send you an item about its grand opening, looking for some free advertising. Interviewing the owner about her background, business plans, hiring expectations, problems with local officials, hopes for the future, and so on, will give you good copy and will avoid giving your readers the impression that you're just doing a favor for a potential advertiser.

Other business topics that make for lively stories are the sale or closing of a local firm, changes in the local employment or real estate markets, the plans and progress of large construction projects, issues related to transportation or public utilities, and stories on the price and availability of fuel. There is a huge variety of consumer information that a newspaper can provide for its readers: seasonal "best buys" and other shopping tips, surveys of prices and services (on the interest rates for home mortgages given by local banks, for example), and warnings of business frauds are just a few such ideas.

Obituaries. We treat obituaries as straight news stories and give them regular news headlines, such as, "Fred Gladstone, Merchant, Is Dead at 81." Another approach is to head a page or a section of a page *Deaths* or *Obituaries,* and then to head each individual obituary with a more cryptic title such as "Fred Gladstone, 81" or "Fred Gladstone Was Local Merchant."

"The saddest news in any small town is death," Henry Hough wrote in *Once More the Thunderer.* "A birth requires only three or four lines in the weekly paper, but an obituary is a chapter in the passing of a generation and challenges the reporter to find words and vision to get everything in." If the person who has died was especially notable—a town official or someone well known or loved by many townspeople—we try either to humanize the notice with our own comments or to invite someone who knew the person well to write a short signed tribute, which we include with its own heading directly after the obituary.

FEATURES

Feature articles can be the most entertaining and original offerings of your paper, if you have some reasonably talented writers on your staff. Usually such articles have as their subjects people or topics that aren't necessarily related to any current news event. Interviews with people of all ages and backgrounds; stories about local history; local slants on regional or national issues—the possibilities are many. But feature stories often require more work and imagination than other kinds of articles. They give the people on your staff the opportunity to write with style and flair, if they have those qualities, and they make your publication more than simply a "news" paper.

News features. A news feature is an article that examines in detail a subject related to a current item of news. Such stories often contain some analysis or conjecture by the writer. They usually require extensive investigation and very careful checking of facts, but they can be among the most rewarding and valuable articles that your newspaper publishes. If, for example, there is a controversy in your community about the awarding of a contract for building a new school, the newspaper could look into the reputations and past practices of the various bidders for the project. Or, if a developer from a distant town proposes to build a new subdivision in your community and asks for variances from local bylaws, the paper could investigate the developer's activities in other towns to see whether he has a reputation for community concern or for self-interest.

Interviews. People are endlessly curious about the stories other people in the community have to tell, and that is why well-written interviews can be among the most popular features in your paper. A good interview can inform, provoke, and entertain; it can also serve as an irreplaceable record of memories of times past. As part of a news story, an interview can provide arresting insights into aspects of the news that might otherwise go unnoticed.

When you call someone to ask for an interview—whether you are looking for a simple answer to a question that has come up in a news story or for a full-blown feature piece—be sure to identify yourself as a writer for the newspaper. From that point on, you are entitled to print the person's responses to your questions. People will often ask you to keep some confidence to yourself, and here you must rely on judgment and experience. Don't be intimidated. If the person says, "I'll talk to you only on condition that this is off the record," try saying no. Many times the person will give in and talk, for his interest in having his point of view reported may win out over his reluctance to be quoted. In any case, you can always go back later and agree to an off-the-record conversation if necessary, but consider this course carefully before taking it. Seasoned reporters walk a precarious path when they balance an exchange of privileged information for the favor of their confidentiality. With an inexperienced reporter, this can lead to a dreadful tangle of pressures and misunderstanding; it is better to make no promises and to play the reporting game straight, at least until you have learned all the rules and seen where some of the traps are.

In your attempts to persuade a reluctant subject to agree to talk with you, the good offices of a mutual friend can sometimes help. It is often an icebreaker, in fact, to bring along someone who knows the subject well to prompt memories and ease conversation, especially with an elderly interviewee.

In general, the best material will emerge from the last five minutes or so of any interview. By this time the subject has relaxed a bit, and may be anxious to conclude the session. If you save your tough questions for the very end, you will find that the answers are more open and revealing than if you had posed the same questions earlier on.

Always use a tape recorder when conducting an interview. Few subjects will object, and those who do can usually be persuaded by pointing out that the tape will make sure you don't misquote them. Take notes during the interview as well, jotting down questions that occur to you while the subject is talking (so you don't forget them), visual observations that will allow you to describe the scene more vividly when you write your article, and general notes about the course of the interview so that you can find your way around in the tape more easily.

The laws regarding taping of telephone conversations vary from state to state. In some, you are required to tell the subject that you are taping the call. Check with the local bar association for advice on this issue.

Columns. There are probably people in your community who could be persuaded to contribute columns to your paper on any of many subjects. Gardening, cooking, hunting and fishing, politics, medicine, law, finance, humor, shopping, travel, birdwatching, sports—these are just some of the topics that might be covered in regular columns by staff or nonstaff writers.

Reviews. Consider devoting a page to reviews of books, plays, concerts, movies, and exhibitions. Your readers will appreciate another intelligent opinion, a perspective on the arts and literature different from that offered by the urban or national media. A delightful fringe benefit of publishing reviews is that you will be able to obtain complimentary books from publishers and tickets to many events. Write on your paper's letterhead to the organization's publicity department to request such courtesies, and send them two tear sheets of the published review. (If you can't get free materials or tickets and you print a review anyway, remember that any costs you incur are tax-deductible. This is an especially useful fact in relation to restaurant reviews; it is perfectly legitimate to deduct the full cost of a restaurant meal if you use it as the basis for writing and publishing a review of the place.)

Calendars and listings. A calendar of local events of all types can be one of the best and easiest ways to build your paper's circulation, especially if there isn't already in your community a single source people can use to find out what's going on and when. Put the calendar in a prominent position, perhaps even on the front page, but in any case in the same spot each week. If the calendar becomes very long and unwieldy, consider breaking it up into two or more separate listings—one for meetings of official town boards, for example, and one for social and cultural events.

School-lunch menus for the coming week, schedules of church services, listings of social service agencies, and schedules of school and local sporting events are other listings you may want to include. We list the names and show times of movies at theaters in our area. In effect, this is free advertising for the theaters; but we find that they are reluctant advertisers anyway, and that some people buy the paper simply for the movie listings. Twenty-five cents, the current newsstand price of the Post, is less in our area than just one or two telephone calls to theaters. And, in exchange for the free listings, most of the theater managers let us go to the movies free whenever we want to.

Classified ads. Publishing free or very inexpensive classified ads (see *Advertising,* page 109) is another way to increase circulation, though you may lose out on some classified advertising revenue. As far as we can tell, our classified pages are the ones most intensely perused by our readers. Many will buy the paper more for its value as a marketplace than as a medium for news.

Out-of-copyright material. Essays, poems, short stories, and articles that are in the public domain are free and can add a touch of history, humor, or style to your paper. The writing of Henry David Thoreau, for example, has often appeared in the Harvard Post. We find his essays to be delightfully written, and his observations are often surprisingly timely.

Check the public library and the historical society for copies of any local newspapers that were published in previous decades or in the nineteenth century. They are invariably a wonderful source of entertaining, enlightening, and free material for your paper.

Filler. It is quite easy—and can be a great deal of fun—to devise your own special features to use as fillers for odd corners of the newspaper. The Harvard Post has had any number of these that have come and gone over the years: the "Press Release of the Week" (the most ridiculous item that came in the mail that week); "It's the Law," which consisted of fascinating excerpts from the often bizarre regulations of the Commonwealth of Massachusetts; crossword puzzles, cryptograms, and double-crostics submitted by readers and staff members; a comic strip invented and drawn by two staff members; a serial novel about small-town life; and even a bogus horoscope column, written by "Omor Ga'rbaj."

EDITORIALS

Reporting the news may be the most important function of your paper, and writing feature stories may allow the most freedom for your writing talents and imagination, but probably the most enjoyable and challenging aspect of the job from the journalist's point of view is making something personal and worthwhile out of the editorial page. It is on this page—one almost always kept free of ads—that the editors, staff, columnists, and readers get a chance to have their say. If you had to be cool and objective in a front-page story you wrote about a proposal to build a new road through town, on the editorial page you can say whatever is on your mind.

Once you start a paper, you may be a little awed by the fact that you now have a forum and an audience; and in a small community it will be no secret whose opinions are being expressed in an editorial. But take the First Amendment seriously and don't be timid about speaking your mind. Even if your readers disagree with you, you can at least give them something to think about, amuse them, make them mad, or prick their consciences.

Some editors seem to have no difficulty in thinking up topics for editorials, whereas others have to rack their brains to come up with appropriate ideas. If you are in the latter group, you might try to solicit guest editorials from local officials, political leaders, and the like. If they are doubtful about their writing abilities, offer to help them with phrasing and editing advice. Even if those you approach turn down your invitation, you will most likely have inspired some good will just by asking.

When you are writing editorials, keep in mind that they need not be constructed solely of opinions. Often the most effective editorials are those that build their conclusions upon a solid structure of documented facts. The more logical and the less emotional your argument, the more likely it is that you will be able to sway the minds of those who do not already agree with you. Even worse than overemotional editorials, however, are those that don't say much of anything. If you get to the end of your editorial and find that it can be summed up by saying, "This issue deserves careful thought," tear it up and start over.

A word about bylines. A byline is simply the name of the author of a story. It usually appears in a contrasting style of type at the beginning of the story, or in some cases at the end. You'll have to decide what kinds of stories you wish to byline and which you don't.

In recent years the trend at most newspapers has been to byline virtually every kind of story—news as well as features and opinion columns. Professional journalists, it is thought, deserve personal recognition for their work. In the early years of the Harvard Post we bylined every article in which the author's personal point of view appeared: features, news features or news analyses, reviews, and columns. We did not byline straight news stories, though; we felt that the editors of a newspaper should take final responsibility for the accuracy of news stories, and that it was up to the editors to make sure that personal opinion didn't appear in the guise of news. Our reporters are part-timers—as most writers on small newspapers are likely to be—who do the work more for their own enjoyment and experience than for the modest amounts they get paid. When townspeople had complaints about the way the Post covered the news, we believed, those complaints should be directed at the editors, not at the reporters. We concluded that not to identify the author of a news story could save the reporter from undeserved harassment or embarrassment.

In recent years, however, we have changed our minds on this issue—partly because our reporting staff has become larger and more experienced. The Post's reporters now have more responsibility for keeping track of and analyzing developments in their news beats. With this responsibility has come greater public visibility. We now use bylines on all substantial news reports.

Editorials usually aren't bylined because they are supposed to reflect the opinion of all the editors. Some papers, though, like the Maine Times, print the initials of the individual writer at the end of each editorial. Many papers run an initialed or signed editorial only when it reflects the minority or dissenting opinion of a staff member.

Letters to the editor. A letters column gives your readers a chance to respond to your editorials, correct or expand upon reports that have appeared in the paper, or comment on matters that interest or infuriate them. The first nasty letter you receive—and it probably won't be long in coming—is sure to be a blow to your journalistic confidence and self-esteem. Encourage your readers to send letters to the paper, though, and try to maintain a liberal policy about publishing them. Watch out for letters that might contain libelous statements, and don't insist upon rebutting each critical letter that comes in. It's your paper, so you'll always have the last word somehow if you want it.

Make sure that the author of each letter identifies himself. We make it a policy to ask for the writer's name, address, and telephone number so we can confirm that he or she is the actual author of the letter and so we can seek permission to revise or delete a portion if we feel it contains libelous, false, or seriously misleading statements. Under certain circumstances, we will agree to withhold the name of the author—usually only if revealing it would expose the person to unnecessary embarrassment or injury. But a strict policy against publication of anonymous letters is essential for your own protection. (When we receive one that seems printworthy we run a message in our classified section, asking the writer to let us know who he is.) You will also have to arrive at a policy on the editing of letters. We believe it is best to correct all errors of spelling and grammar and to try to assist the letter-writer's attempt to get his opinions across in direct and economical language. It is best to check with the writer by phone, however, before making any significant changes.

There are sure to be articulate, impassioned, or simply eccentric people in your community who have criticisms, suggestions, opinions, or anecdotes that deserve to be heard. A lively page of letters to the editor is an unmistakable hallmark of every outstanding newspaper.

PHOTOGRAPHS AND ARTWORK

The offset printing process makes the reproduction of black-and-white photographs and artwork a relatively simple matter (see *Printing,* pages 37–39). They should become an important part of the overall design of your paper, contributing to its visual interest and impact for the entertainment and information of your readers.

A few thoughts on choosing photographs to publish:

¶ Make it a goal to find and use at least one good photograph on your front page every issue. It doesn't have to depict a particular news event; a candid shot of a person in town or a seasonal landscape can add a nice touch to the front page.

¶ Try to avoid using too many photographs of people or groups of people simply standing and looking straight at the camera. Encourage your photographers to catch people actually *doing* things.

¶ Use photographs that have a good range of tonal values, from white to black. Photographs that have a uniform tone of grey throughout, without much contrast, will be difficult for your printcr to rcproducc well. On the other hand, beware of photographs that are divided into areas of pure black and pure white. The halftone screen used by the printer puts a pattern of dots in even the whitest and the darkest areas. And you'll also make your printer's job easier if you use photographs that have similar tonal ranges, as he may be able to "gang" them—shoot several together at the same time—without having to change camera exposure.

¶ You'll often find that scenes photographed from a low angle seem to produce better, more lively shots.

If you're not a good photographer yourself, stay on the alert for any photographers in your community who might be eager to take advantage of your paper as a medium in which to display their work. Ask the proprietor of the local camera shop for the names of amateur photographers who like to develop and print their own pictures. Someone who can take candid, authentic photographs of local people and places will prove invaluable. But be sure always to credit the photographer, either at the end of the caption or in small type adjacent to the picture. Do this even if the photograph is an old one that you have used before and saved in your file. The photograph belongs to the person who took it; he or she should be consulted, credited, and paid each time it is used.

Keep in mind the distinction between *line* drawings and *continuous tone* art. Black-and-white line drawings can often simply be pasted into place on a camera-ready page. If you have artists or cartoonists contributing to your paper, encourage them to work in pen and ink, which is easy to reproduce. Art with shades of grey, though, has to be treated just like a photograph and shot by the printer through a screen. With both line drawings and continuous tone artwork you can always paste a *blackout* into your laid-out page as if it were a photograph, and have your printer enlarge or reduce the illustration to a different size from the original. (See *Printing,* pages 37–39.)

Remember: your goods in trade consist almost entirely of various kinds of information—in the form of articles, photographs, and artwork. You'll earn an audience for your paper, and keep it, if you can provide information your readers can't get elsewhere and if you can present it in a form they can enjoy and depend on. Your goal is to make your readers addicts of your newspaper—so dependent upon it that they can't get through the week without poring over its every word and illustration.

The difference between a great news-paper picture (left) and an inexcus-ably boring one (below) is action, emotion, angle.

COPYRIGHT

Under the Copyright Act of 1976, copyright protection for all "original works of authorship" exists automatically from the moment of their creation. It is not necessary for you to register your publication formally with the Copyright Office in order to prevent other people from using any of the material in it without your permission. To secure all of the legal rights that are available, however, it is important to include a notice of copyright in each issue. Doing this is quite simple.

The notice of copyright consists of three elements: (1) the word "Copyright," or the abbreviation "Copr.," or the symbol ©; (2) the year of publication; and (3) the name of the copyright owner. These three elements must appear together; for example, © Eliza Miller 1983, or, Copyright 1983 by The Harvard Post. The notice should appear either on the title page, or on the first page of text, or under the title heading. If you put the notice in your masthead (which is usually on the editorial page), the masthead must also include the complete title of the newspaper and any other elements needed to identify the work, such as the volume, number, and date of the issue.

For most small newspapers, simply including a copyright notice in each issue will afford ample protection from copyright infringement. To comply fully with the Copyright Act, it is also necessary to send two copies of each issue to the Library of Congress. These may be sent by second-class mail, and no accompanying note of explanation is needed.

There are a few additional rights, though, that may be secured by actually registering with the Copyright Office. This involves filling out Copyright Form SE and sending it in with two copies of the issue and a $10 fee. Each issue of a periodical must be registered separately; this means that for a weekly newspaper copyright registration costs more than $500 per year.

Whether or not you decide to copyright your newspaper, take care not to infringe upon the copyrights of others. You must obtain permission and, usually, pay a fee before reproducing copyrighted material. The law stipulates not only civil but also criminal liability for copyright infringement.

For more information about copyright, write to the Register of Copyrights, Copyright Office, Library of Congress, Washington, D.C. 20559, and ask for a copy of Circular R1, "Copyright Basics."

The editors and reporters on a weekly newspaper have one big advantage over their counterparts on a daily—time. Take advantage of the fact that you don't have a deadline every day by providing more background and detail in your news stories. Call people, gather and use more quotations, look into relevant ordinances and laws, investigate the history of issues that are discussed at meetings. While the small newspaper has to guard against articles that are too long-winded or contain superfluous information, it can give its readers a better, more complete understanding of an issue or event just by including more detail and background.

"[I]t's hard to get someone to write freely and naturally nowadays, unless you take him young," Henry Beetle Hough wrote in 1950, in *Once More the Thunderer:*

> Most of the sophisticated feel they must follow an adaptation of *Time* style or else write in a stutter.
>
> But we believe it is still deep in the nature of writing men and women to be articulate, even fluent, and the opposite only seems to be true because of limited opportunities. To sharpen a story into vivid and economical language is not the same thing as discarding most of the values and seeking to represent them through a few clipped sentences. Yet in many of the cities scattered across America there are daily newspapers for which concision is no longer enough; stories cannot be told any longer, but only symbolized. . . . The first chapter of Genesis, for all its beauty and economy, is a dangerous precedent for the news-paperman; one must not forget that the world would have liked a fuller account, even with stories of description and first hand experience as told by eyewitnesses.

3 Editing

WHERE DOES A NEWSPAPER DERIVE ITS PERSONALITY? What makes one paper merely a bulletin board and another a compelling mix of news and entertainment? Though the contents of all newspapers are essentially the same in nature—news, features, editorials, illustrations—each one's character and presentation are almost completely determined by the kind of editing that has shaped them into finished form.

It is easy to imagine the editor's job as reactive; and it is true that to respond to the tremendous amount of material that might be included in any one edition requires a good deal of time and energy. The editor must sort out what is important news and what can be relegated to stray corners; must plan the mix of material so that a given issue is neither too dry nor too fluffy; and must work carefully with mountains of paper to impose standards of accuracy, fairness, and style on each article. Surely that is enough to ask of any small newspaper editor.

But the best editors go one step further. To generate ideas for the real stories that lie hidden behind the routine news; to plan and execute a series of articles that focuses on an important subject; to provide leadership to staff writers in matters of journalistic integrity—these are the ways an editor can turn an already good small newspaper into a superb one. To exercise these powers is a creative, not a reactive, task. It can make the newspaper an important force in the community; and it can set a standard equaling that of the best newspapers of any size.

In fact, your job as editor of a small paper will combine elements of every stereotypical idea the public has of what an editor does. You will be the shirtsleeved city editor, making important and powerful decisions amid the chaos of ringing phones and last-minute news flashes. You will be the merciless butcher of flabby writing, rendering muscular news reports and pithy headlines from the least promising material. And you will be the bespectacled drone with dictionary and style manual at your elbow, blue-penciling copy until it is as close to perfect as you can make it. In this chapter we will describe what you should know as you go about doing all three of these tasks at once, which is both the peculiar burden and the pleasure of every small newspaper editor.

THE BIG PICTURE

Your first responsibility as editor is to plan the issue—or the next few issues—that lies ahead. You will probably already have a good sense of what news will be coming up from official meetings and community events scheduled in the week to come. You have assigned reporters to cover these events and have given them deadlines by which they must turn in their work; you have asked photographers to take pictures where appropriate. You also have planned a feature article, or perhaps two main features, for the issue; and you have a good idea of what regular columns you can expect from your stable of contributors. In addition, you know that you can expect reams of press releases from every conceivable interest group to come in the mail today and tomorrow.

It is easy at this point to figure that you have the whole community covered. In fact, this is where you can exercise the most skill and judgment in the planning of your issue. Will the school board and the finance committee both be reacting to the same piece of news—say, the announcement of deep cuts in state aid to education—in their meetings this week? The story should be treated as a separate article, combining facts and statements from the two meetings—not buried in the reports of the meetings. Is there a need for a clear explanation of the zoning laws that are causing a ruckus between that housing developer and the planning board? Assign a background piece to be included as a sidebar next to the main article. Are you looking at a boring week—no important meetings, no big news? Don't wish for a fire at Town Hall; instead, call ten prominent people in town and ask their opinions of some news development covered last week, or generate an article on the local effects of some broader issue in the state or national press. Your skill in coming up with good slants on the great mass of information that assaults your readers every day will result in a paper that is lively and interesting even after the dullest week.

It will not take you long to realize that this kind of creative planning is the first thing to go as the weeks rush towards their deadlines. You will probably be so exhausted by the things you absolutely have to do that there will be very little time left for contemplation or creative thought. That is why it is wise to schedule regular staff meetings—we have ours once a month—to look over the last few issues and talk about their strong points and weaknesses, to come up with new ideas for the issues to come, to assign features that will require extra time on the part of the reporter, and to address whatever problems staff writers are having with their assignments. It is in the exchange and flow of ideas that the best stories are born—and your staff will be revitalized by their participation in this planning process.

If you are directly competing with another newspaper that serves the same community, this kind of creating editing can give you a distinct edge. The newspaper that develops a reputation for reporting real news and informed opinion will inevitably win out over a competitor that serves merely as a bulletin board for the same old community events.

The job of your reporters is to provide you with as much information as they can gather. Your job as editor is to sift through that information and decide which of it is fit to print. When your reporters are being pressured to keep something "off the record," you will have to decide whether the request is legitimate or not; when you are on the trail of a hot story that involves your biggest advertiser, your judgment on whether to proceed will be necessary. The best editors balance a myriad of factors in making decisions like this for every issue; and none escapes without some embarrassing slip-ups. There are, however, some important guidelines that have proved helpful in figuring out what "all the news that's fit to print" means in your particular case.

Open meetings. Public business should be conducted in public; and official reluctance to acknowledge this often extends down to the grassroots. If yours is the first good newspaper in your community, you may face public officials who habitually assume that *they* are the ones who should decide what the public should know about what goes on at their meetings. They may tell you in the middle of a meeting that what they are saying is "off the record"—without realizing that what goes on in a public meeting is the public's business and can be reported. Or they may even attempt to bar reporters from a meeting.

Find out what laws in your state govern the meetings of local boards and committees. Such "sunshine" or open-meeting laws have been enacted or tightened up in many states in recent years. In most cases they define specific reasons for which officials may meet in closed, or "executive," sessions. Once the officials in your community are aware that your paper is paying attention not only to *what* governmental business is being conducted, but also to *how* it is being conducted, the quality of local political debate and activity may significantly improve.

Ticklish situations. Especially once you begin digging into matters that are beyond the scope of routine committee meetings, you will often find yourself with ticklish situations to resolve. Should you put the story about the bank official indicted for embezzlement on the front page, when the bank is your biggest advertiser? Do you really need to include in the police report the news that Benson N. Hedges was arrested for drunken driving, when he has come to you with tears in his eyes and pled that to do so would ruin his corporate career? Hester Prynne agreed to that interview with the greatest reluctance, and now insists that she be allowed to read the story before you print it to see that you have it right. What do you say to her?

The answers to such questions are seldom simple. You must report the news fairly and objectively; and in the case of the police news, for example, that means denying special favors even if the drunken driver is your closest friend. The laws in some states protect juvenile offenders from disclosure of their names in the press (find out if this is the case in your state); aside from that, police arrest reports and court records are public information. If you are legally free to publish the names of youthful offenders, you will face some difficult decisions. Another sensitive question is whether to print the names of the victims of crime, particularly rape. Editors' opinions differ on these issues; the important thing is for you to decide on a policy and then stick to it.

The best policy is to yield to no pressures; but at the same time take special care when reporting sensitive stories that every fact is double-checked and that you have not sensationalized the news. Usually the drunken driver has been dreading the sight of his disgrace splashed all over the front page, and is brought down to earth when he realizes that his name is simply a minor note in a routine story.

Requests like Hester Prynne's, to "check over" your story before it goes into print, can be dealt with in a different manner. Never turn over a story to someone not on the newspaper staff to read before it goes into the paper; to do so would be to permit a subtle form of censorship, and would undermine your newspaper's independence and set a dangerous precedent. It is all right, though—and sometimes even crucial—to call the subject of an interview and check the facts and opinions you have attributed to him or her. This can be done in an informal way and can benefit you both. Even if the person says, "Oh, I didn't mean it to sound like that," and you are forced to give up some juicy quotation, you will often gather some other material that is just as usable as the person explains what it was she really wanted to say. And you will have gained a measure of trust that will help your reputation for fairness and accuracy.

This is not to say that public figures should always be allowed to change their minds later about the things they may have told a reporter in an unguarded moment. But there is no need for you to take on the callous attitude of the hard-nosed big-city editor who pays no attention to the human feelings and failings of those who appear in the news. Everyone says things that he doesn't mean, and sometimes fails to express himself clearly. Why shouldn't he be given a chance to correct the record before the damage is done?

When it comes to advertisers in the news, you will have a special problem. Of course, if an advertiser's name comes up in a news context— such as the police news, or the affairs of some public body—you are obliged to treat it the same way as any other person's name, being sure that your facts are correct and contacting the named individual to obtain a comment. The embezzling bank official, then, will end up with her name in the paper. But when it comes to investigative reporting, you have more discretion in pursuing news; and your decisions will necessarily be influenced by the degree to which you depend on that firm's business. If yours is a brand-new, struggling paper with just three large advertisers, think carefully before you embark on a controversial investigation of one of them. Can the paper survive without those advertising dollars? Can the investigation wait until the paper is more solidly grounded in the community? You do neither yourself nor your readers a favor by putting yourself out of business.

This situation is quite rare, though. In general, you will find that the more real reporting you do, the more readers you will have, and if you have the readers the advertisers will soon follow. Decide which issues are truly important to follow up; assess the potential damage that can be done to you or to others by your reporting; and then proceed with every attention to accuracy and objectivity. If your goal is really governmental or social reform, you will soon discover an interesting side effect of this approach. Because you will have earned a reputation for taking on the tough issues, sometimes you will be able to bring about reform merely by asking pointed questions—even if you never print the story. Those in power will know that you *might* publish it, and they will be more likely to stay away from dirty dealing for fear you will find out.

SUBSTANTIVE EDITING

After the plan for an issue is fairly complete and stories have begun to pile up on the desk, your first task is the substantive editing of the material that comes in from the newspaper staff. This entails a meticulous check of each story for its objectivity, its completeness, and its factual accuracy. Has the reporter telephoned Mr. Mephisto, who has been indicted for running a child pornography ring, to solicit a comment on the story? (Making such calls may not be easy, but it is essential at least to provide the opportunity for the subject of the story to respond if he so desires; and in any case he will appreciate being forewarned that his name is going to show up in this week's paper.) Do the figures add up in the article on the school budget? Is there someone else whose opinion should be solicited about the news that your town is being redistricted by the legislature? In the rush to deadline it is easy to overlook such matters, but your attention to them at this point makes the difference between a good newspaper and a mediocre one.

Be especially attentive to the reports of the meetings of official boards, particularly if you are working with inexperienced reporters. Too often such stories take on the flavor of the minutes of the meeting; they begin at the beginning and take the reader blow by blow through to the end. Work with your reporters to help them identify instead the most important thing that took place and state it clearly in the lead paragraph. Impose some unity within the article; if the selectmen talked about three important issues at their last meeting, you should probably have three shorter articles with separate headlines rather than combining them all under a more general head. Keep your eye open for signs that an article should be combined with some news from another story to make a more comprehensive whole.

It is also your job to ensure that the proper background is given when a news story appears. Try not to assume that your readers have perfect recall of all that has gone before; remind them with a succinct background sentence or two towards the beginning of the article. If you use abbreviations or acronyms that are not widely understood, spell out the full name the first time it appears in the story, giving the abbreviated form in parentheses immediately after—for example, the Department of Housing and Urban Development (HUD). If you pay attention to such details in your substantive editing, your reporters will soon learn what you expect of them and your task will be made much easier.

Watch for material that could be pulled from the body of the story and presented in a more graphically appealing way as a *sidebar,* a subsidiary story set apart within the main article by a box or other device. Comparative figures, reactions from prominent citizens, and explanations of state or local regulations pertaining to the issues being discussed could all be treated in this way.

Keep a sharp eye out for *attribution* of statements in all reporting—that is, making clear whose opinions are being expressed. It is easy to let something like this slip by: "Mr. Smith said that the construction of a new fire station should begin this year. Each year's delay will cost an additional $10,000." Because it is unattributed, the statement in the second sentence appears to be the opinion of the newspaper. Adding the phrase "he said" to the sentence eliminates the confusion—but only if that is really what Smith said. If Smith didn't say it, who did? Think twice about publishing any opinion, allegation, prediction, or personal remark in a news story if you cannot provide a source for it. (More on attribution appears in *Content,* page 12.)

Libel. A published statement may be judged libelous if it questions the integrity or virtue of a living person, thus exposing him or her to public ridicule and damaging his reputation, or causing him financial loss. Newspaper editors must constantly be watchful for such statements, even though the courts in recent years have been reluctant to hand down libel judgments against newspapers in all but the most extreme cases.

Study the libel laws in your state and consult a friendly lawyer before publishing anything you think may be libelous. In general, your defenses against a libel suit are (1) to prove that the defamatory statements were true; (2) to show that the statements were privileged, that is, part of any public or official proceeding or document; or (3) to show that the statements were made in good faith (that is, without knowledge of their falsity) and without malice. Newspapers are generally allowed great freedom in printing opinions and even personal attacks on government officials, celebrities, and other public figures. You can be sued, however, for invasion of privacy if you cause embarrassment or injury to an ordinary citizen when there is no compelling reason for the public to know the details of what you have reported.

Satire, both in the form of writing and in the form of the editorial cartoon, can be one of the most effective and even devastating ways to express strong opinions in a newspaper. The courts have almost always held that satire is protected by the First Amendment guarantee of free speech, but you should still exercise care in using it. For one thing, an alarmingly large percentage of your readers will take everything you write quite literally; therefore, if you enjoy writing with tongue in cheek, be prepared to have someone try to take a swing at it occasionally. Reviews are another area in which wide latitude is given but restraint should be practiced. If your newspaper publishes reviews, by all means give your reviewers the freedom to praise or damn as they see fit, but don't let them go overboard. If your reviewer writes that he was poisoned by the food at the Greasy Spoon Family Restaurant, you'd better be able to prove in court that he was.

The best precaution against libel is to check your paper carefully, *before* you take it to the printer, for all defamatory, irresponsible, and anonymous or otherwise unattributed statements. Another precaution is simply not to have any money; poor people are very rarely sued for damages. If you do have money, and you also like to criticize and stir up trouble, perhaps you ought to take out libel insurance.

COPY EDITING

After you have checked an article for substantive problems—angle, objectivity, thoroughness, and the like—it is time to turn your attention to the writing itself. The process of revising for matters of grammar, consistency, and style is called copy editing; it is an art that seems to depend at least as much on having an ear for language as it does on knowledge of specific grammatical rules. A good copy editor is one with a passion for words used well, and the patience to check carefully every instance that is in doubt. This means caring whether the subject agrees with the verb, whether two words could be used in place of ten, whether a vivid, active verb is used rather than a bland, passive one.

Flabby, wordy writing is probably the most common affliction of modern newspapers, yet it is not always easy to see what it is that makes a sentence dull. Associated Press editor Rene J. Cappon gives the following example in the book *The Newspaper,* published by the National Newspaper Foundation:

> Verbosity is not the same as length. A 2,000-word article can be succinct, a 200-word short grossly overwritten. The following sentence, from a story about one of California's perennial brush fires, seems succinct enough: *Five rescue ambulances stood by to rush the injured to nearby hospitals.* But eight of these twelve words are unemployed. Ambulances usually rescue, they don't dawdle, they carry the injured rather than the healthy, and they seldom hunt for remoter hospitals. "Five ambulances stood by" was all the writer needed.

If you are the kind of editor who is better at the substantive than the mechanical side of editing, it would be worthwhile to develop someone else on your staff to be the copy editor. No matter how impressive the content of an article, it will lose power if presented in awkward or incorrect prose.

Copy editors have at their disposal a number of useful standard reference books. We rely on the University of Chicago *Manual of Style*, the *Associated Press Style Book,* and *The Elements of Style,* by William S. Strunk, Jr. and E. B. White; and on *The American Heritage Dictionary*

COPY EDITING MARKS

Mark	Meaning	Example
⌐ or ¶	Paragraph	⌐The worst blizzard to hit
/	Lower case	Harvard in recorded /History
◯	Contract to figures	left (thirty) inches of snow on
or ◯	Spell out	town streets yesterday. (300)
|	Insert space	years since|the town's founding
∽	Transpose	have (seen not) so much snow"
≡	Capitalize	said Highway superintendent Bill
ℐ	Delete and close up	Boonehead, leafing through a copy
___	Italicize	of the Farmer's Almanac after a
⊙	Insert period	night of work supervising plows⊙
～	Boldface	Extra Help Put On
≠∧	Insert hyphen	All six part⁼time employees
....	Stet, let it stand	of the highway department came

Mark	Meaning	Mark	Meaning
ℒ	Delete	═	Align horizontally
⊂⊃	Close up; delete space	‖	Align vertically
ℐ	Delete and close up	∽	Transpose
#	Insert space	◯	Spell out; contract to figures
¶	Begin new paragraph	....	Let it stand
no ¶	Run paragraphs together	∧	Insert comma
▢	Move type one em from left or right	∨	Insert apostrophe (or single quotation mark)
⊐	Move right	∨∨	Insert quotation marks
⊏	Move left	⊙ or ⊗	Insert period
⊐⊏	Center	=	Insert hyphen
⊓	Move up	─M	Insert em dash
⊔	Move down	─N	Insert en dash

with its endlessly absorbing notes on usage. Style books vary, however, on many questions, and it can be time-consuming to flip through them again and again to resolve commonly encountered problems; so it is a good idea to start your own newspaper style book. This can be a simple spiral binder with a page for each letter; enter in it your standard usage for capitalization, punctuation, and spelling questions that you frequently face. Is it "Women's Club" or "Woman's Club"? Does Silvio Amaretto prefer to see his name in print as Si, since everyone calls him that? The abbreviations A.M. and P.M. are most properly set in small caps, but you don't have small caps on your typesetter; whether you decide on lower case (a.m.) or upper case (A.M.)—both are acceptable—you should at least be consistent. Such seemingly minor matters really do make a difference, though your readers may be only vaguely aware of it.

The copy editor should also keep a sharp eye out for factual errors, misspelled names, matters of attribution, and other problems that may have slipped by a previous editor. And if this has not already been done, the copy editor should insert subheads into extended passages of text to break up the long columns of grey.

Errors and corrections. Even the best newspapers make errors. Correct your mistakes promptly and in print, placing the correction in a prominent position and heading it clearly. Your readers know you're fallible. They should also know that you are honest enough to acknowledge your mistakes and set the record straight.

WRITING HEADLINES

When the copy has been edited for substance and for style, the editor should write a headline for it. It's good to draft a head even before the article goes to the typesetter, though final headlines will be determined later when the copy has been positioned on the layout sheets. (See *Design and Layout,* pages 86–88.) Writing a preliminary headline at this stage takes advantage of your having just read the article, so its main points are fresh in your mind. You can have it set directly above the article in regular body-copy type, and later you can modify it for length and specify a type style.

Headlines should be written in the "present historical" tense or the future tense. *Phone Company Raises Rates for Harvard Customers* means that the rates have already been raised. *Garden Club Will Hear Speaker on Land Use* is an example of the proper use of the future tense. The headline on a news article should be terse and understandable and should summarize the main point of the story without repeating the first sentence. Even in an article that might seem to require it, don't use the admonitory tone—*Shovel Out Your Mailbox, Postmaster Warns* is better than just *Shovel Out Your Mailbox.*

A good headline is specific, clear, and accurate. It uses key words to convey information that absolutely must be in the head if the reader is to learn what the story is about. It does not make broad generalizations that are unsubstantiated by the story. In headlines at least as much as in articles, attribution is crucial: *Chemicals in Pond Cause Cancer* is unacceptable, while *Chemicals in Pond Cause Cancer, Basch Says* is fine because it attributes the assertion to the person who made it. Don't use unnecessary words, but don't go to the opposite extreme and fill your headlines with jargon or obscure abbreviations for the sake of saving space.

It is all too easy to write a libelous headline over a story that is perfectly correct, simply by trying too hard to cut out words. If the police arrest someone in an assault case, *Cops Nab Thug* is libelous; the suspect has been arrested, not convicted. Here is a place where "headlinese" can get you into serious legal trouble.

Writing headlines is a serious business, but it can also be a lot of fun. Especially in the case of feature articles, headlines can provide room for wit, poetic phrases, and the kind of imaginative writing that is one of the great satisfactions of editing a newspaper. Two writers are better than one in the headline game, we have learned; and five or six can give rise to a session of hilarity that ends in the perfect headline.

By far the best book to read on the subject of headlines is *Headlines and Deadlines* by New York Times editors Robert E. Garst and Theodore M. Bernstein. A thorough reading of this entertaining and instructive manual will teach you far more about the art of writing succinct headlines than we could hope to include here.

Teaser heads. Occasionally a "teaser" head before the main headline will effectively capture the reader's eye. Such a head can consist of a short quotation from the body of the article (*"I Didn't Say That"* before *Angry Selectmen Picket Newspaper Office*), or a characterizing phrase (*Teapot Tempest* before *Woman's Club Garden Party Rained Out Again.*)

4 Printing

YOU CAN PRODUCE A SMALL NEWSPAPER without owning or knowing how to run a printing press; but in order to prepare a newspaper for reproduction you have to understand the principles of *offset printing,* especially what the process enables you to do and what it prevents you from doing. Offset printing combines the use of photography in the preparation of materials for print with the use of lithography—which is based on the simple fact that oily ink and water don't mix—during the actual printing process.

Traditional *letterpress printing* involves setting metal type and making zinc engravings of photographs and illustrations. These materials are then arranged in a metal form, placed in the press, coated with ink, and impressed directly onto a sheet of paper. The principles involved are exactly those devised in the fifteenth century by Johann Gutenberg. Refined considerably since then, letterpress printing was until the last few decades the most common means of printing newspapers.

Offset printing, though, does away with the metal type and engravings used on a letterpress. What makes the process especially useful and attractive for someone producing a small newspaper is that the preparation of materials for printing can take place at a location remote from the press. You don't need a large Linotype machine, which is messy to operate; and instead of preparing bulky and extremely heavy forms of metal type, all you have to provide for the printer are pages that he can photograph. To oversimplify somewhat, anything that can be photographed in two dimensions by the printer can be reproduced in print by means of offset printing.

The actual work of arranging and affixing type and illustrations on white layout pages (called "flats" or "boards") so that they can be photographed is called *pasteup*. When a page is pasted up as you want it to appear in print, it's *camera-ready*—that is, ready for the printer to photograph it and make a negative of the image that has the same dimensions as the desired finished page. The large camera used for this purpose employs a lens with almost no depth of field; this makes it possible to reduce or enlarge camera-ready copy so that a negative—and thus a final printed image—smaller or larger than the original can be produced.

The negative is then placed on top of a thin, flat metal plate, usually made of aluminum, that has been coated with a photosensitive emulsion. The plate is covered with the negative and then exposed to bright light; light reaches the plate only through the transparent portions of the negative—

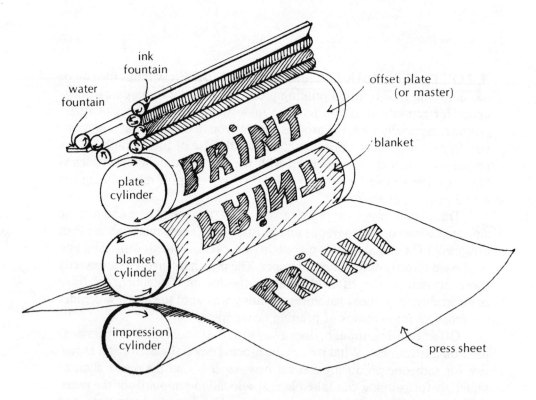

How an offset press works: the engraved metal plate is attached to the plate cylinder, and the printed image is offset to the blanket cylinder and finally to paper.

that is, only through the original images you want to reproduce. Next, the printer washes the plate in a developer, which removes the emulsion from the unexposed areas of the plate, making them more receptive to a coating of water. Then a lacquer is applied, which makes the exposed areas of the plate more receptive to ink.

The metal plate is finally attached to a cylinder on the printing press. When the press begins to roll, other cylinders on the machine coat the plate first with a thin layer of water, then with a coating of ink. The unexposed surfaces of the plate, remember, reject the ink. The inked image on the plate is then transferred, or "offset," to a rubber-covered "blanket" cylinder. Finally, the image is transferred from the blanket cylinder onto a sheet of paper, the original metal plate never having made contact with the paper. And that's the way all offset presses work.

It's important to remember that the printer's camera will detect and reproduce anything on a sheet of copy it sees as black against white. Black type, when pasted up, will appear in sharp contrast to the white paper onto which it is pasted, and the camera will crisply reproduce it on the negative. But the camera also sees most other dark colors as black. Thus, fingerprints, smudges, globs of rubber cement, red pencil marks, and coffee stains will be picked up by the camera, as well as the type and illustrations you want reproduced. The printer can clean up many of these sorts of inadvertent reproducible marks after he has prepared the negative by the process of *opaquing*. He uses a fast-drying liquid to touch up the negative wherever small unwanted transparent areas occur. There is no substitute for clean pasteup work, though; the printer should not be expected to opaque dozens of extraneous marks on each negative.

The copy camera will not do a good job detecting light blue or green, violet, light grey, yellow, and other light colors. Because the camera doesn't detect light blue at all, you will be able to write on and mark up your camera-ready copy with light blue pens and pencils without fear of seeing those marks reproduced.

Line copy, continuous tone copy, and halftones. If you simply pasted a photograph into camera-ready copy, and the printer then shot the whole page, including the photograph, the type portion of the page would be reproduced clearly; the picture, though, would probably end up looking smudged and indistinct, its darker portions appearing as dark black, its light areas all white, with no gradation of grey tones in between.

Offset copy cameras can't accurately reproduce materials that have a gradation of color tones, so-called *continuous tone copy,* such as photographs, pencil sketches, and paintings. These materials have to be treated differently from *line copy*—type and such illustrations as pen-and-ink drawings—when being prepared for printing. To reproduce continuous tone copy, commonly called *halftones,* you have to take an extra step in preparing the copy for the printer, and the printer has to take an extra step in the preparation of the negative from which he will make a printing plate. The effect of these steps, as we will see, is to create on the printed page the illusion of gradations of grey when in fact only small but distinct areas of black and white are being printed.

First, you must decide where on a given page you want to put a halftone illustration and what size you want it to be. (See pages 97–98 for a discussion of sizing illustrations.) Then you simply cut a piece of black, dark red, or orange paper to that size and paste it into place on the page you are laying out, creating what is commonly termed a *blackout* or *knockout.* The preferred, but most expensive, material for this purpose is the dark red acetate called Rubylith; we generally use cheaper and altogether adequate black or orange paper, though.

When photographed by the printer, the blacked-out area produces a corresponding transparent area, called a *window,* in the negative. What the printer does in reproducing a halftone is to make another smaller negative which he affixes onto the large negative to fill up the window. He takes the original photograph or artwork and places over it a *screen,* a sheet of acetate etched with very fine lines at right angles, usually 100 or fewer lines to the inch for newspaper halftones. The screen separates the light reflected from the various tones in the illustration into thousands of little dots of varying sizes. The resulting printed image has larger dots where the original halftone is darker and smaller dots where the original has lighter tones. Thus the appearance of shades of grey is produced, while the printed image in fact consists of thousands of tiny areas of black and white.

If you provide high-quality black-and-white photographs to your printer—pictures that aren't uniformly grey and don't have too much contrast—he should be able to give you good reproductions. Avoid using photographs cut out of other newspapers; they have already been screened once. Screened a second time, such halftones will be distorted by so-called moire patterns when reproduced. Also avoid color photographs, which usually translate poorly into black and white because of the camera's inability to see certain colors while others are seen as black. Sometimes a color photograph will come out all right, but watch out for certain sure signs of trouble—for example, a red object against a dark background, or a light blue object against a light green background.

Advertisers will sometimes do you a favor by supplying you with a *velox,* a halftone illustration that has already been photographed through a

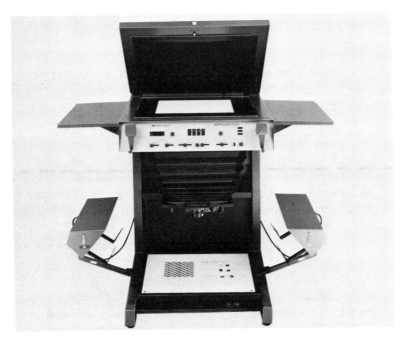

A photostat camera.

very coarse screen. Veloxes can be pasted directly onto a camera-ready page as line copy. Because of the coarse dot pattern, though, veloxes do not provide particularly sharp reproductions.

If you are working with a printer who is not giving you very good picture reproduction, or if you have so many enlarged or reduced illustrations and photographs in every issue that your print run is unacceptably delayed or your printing bills are inflated by extra camera charges, you should consider buying a *photostat camera*. With this machine you can make your own enlargements and reductions of both line art and halftones and you will have much greater control over their quality. At the Harvard Post we bought such a camera several years ago, and it has been well worth the investment. Our ads look better because we are able to enlarge type beyond the capability of our typesetting system; we can see exactly how pictures will reproduce both in ads and editorial copy; and we are even able to make a modest sum by making photostats for outside clients. The Agfa Gevaert Repromaster 2001 camera we bought has a list price of $5,595, and you will have to spend a few hundred dollars more on a processor; but it is possible to obtain substantial discounts on the camera through certain dealers. The Repromaster 2001 is a sturdy, reliable, easy-to-use machine, but there are several other makes and models of photostat cameras on the market for less money, and used equipment is available as well. One note: you will need a darkroom space of at least seven feet by six feet to accommodate such a camera.

Color. The use of a second color in your newspaper can add much to its visual impact and attractiveness; but it also adds to the time and expense of producing a small newspaper, and those are primary considerations. From the printer's point of view, printing a second color is a relatively simple matter. Typically, in the production of a small paper, the second color is used on only a few pages—the front and back pages or the centerfold, for instance—so the printer uses the different color ink on just one unit of the press and on one plate. Usually he will charge a flat extra amount for the additional color, because it involves extra press cleanup time and the production of an additional plate.

You'll also have to prepare more complicated camera-ready mechanicals for the printer. The basic white layout sheet will be prepared in the usual way, but will contain only the copy to be reproduced in black (or whatever the primary color is). All material to be printed in the second color must be affixed to a transparent overlay sheet, usually of tissue or acetate. Corner crop-marks on both the background and overlay sheets insure that the two layouts line up properly.

You will have to decide whether the added effect of a second color in your paper is worth the additional time and money you'll have to spend.

A concise but informative guide to the essentials of offset printing, covering in greater detail some of the matters discussed in this chapter, is Clifford Burke's *Printing It.*

FINDING A PRINTER

Sheetfed and web presses. Offset printing presses come in a wide variety of sizes and designs, each suited to particular kinds of printing. An important distinction to keep in mind is that between *sheetfed* and *web* presses. Sheetfed presses print rectangular sheets of paper and come in many sizes: 10 inches by 15 inches, 11 inches by 17 inches, 17 by 22, and on up, the dimensions denoting the size plate the press can hold. Some of the smaller presses, such as the famous Addressograph-Multigraph Multilith, are relatively inexpensive and are useful for printing brochures, stationery, newsletters, and the like. Books, which are usually printed 16, 32, or 64 pages to a sheet, are often produced on larger sheetfed presses.

These days, though, newspapers are almost always printed on web presses, large multi-unit machines that print not on single rectangular sheets but on long, wide rolls of paper. The continuous sheet running through the press forms the "web." A web press designed for newspaper use can print papers in both compact-size (or "tabloid") and full-size (or "metro") formats; it can print both sides of the sheet at the same time, print certain pages of the paper in more than one color, and collate and fold the paper, delivering each copy at the end of the press ready to read.

Web presses are complicated and temperamental machines that require experienced operators. But the most compelling reason why someone starting a small newspaper shouldn't consider buying his own press is the likely cost: even a relatively small web offset publication press could cost $150,000 or more. In order to make such a machine pay for itself its owner must keep the press operating as much as possible; but your paper will probably require less than an hour of printing time for each issue.

It shouldn't be difficult to find a printer in your area who has a web press that isn't being used to capacity and that he'd like more work for. The best place to start looking for a printer is at other nearby newspapers that might be looking for work for their presses at times when they aren't busy. And then there are other printers with web presses who may not produce publications of their own, but simply have a regular schedule of newspapers they produce for different customers during the week. You may have to go far afield in your search for a printer, but it's probably worth talking with as many as you can before deciding on who will print your paper. You may find that the better price and service offered by a more distant printer justify the money and time spent in additional travel. And, to be honest, you may have a hard time at first persuading a large-scale printing operation to take you on, particularly if your circulation—and thus your press run—is very small.

Questions to ask. Once you've found a few printers, these are some of the matters you'll want to question each of them about:

Size. Find out what size newspaper is most convenient and economical for him to print. Newsprint is customarily manufactured in rolls that are 31 or 35 inches wide. The smaller width produces a small-format newspaper with a page size of about 11½ inches by 15 inches; the wider paper yields a page size of about 11½ inches by 17 inches. Some printers stock only one width or the other, so the page size of your publication may well hinge on what width paper your printer uses.

Number of pages. Find out also the maximum number of pages the printer's press can handle, even though you're not likely to exceed that limit right away. The number of pages that the press is able to produce almost always has to be a multiple of four; if it's your goal to put out a 32-page issue someday (even though you may start out with only eight- or twelve-page editions), and the printer you choose can print a maximum of 24 pages, you may eventually find yourself having to change printers.

Quality. Of course, you will also want to examine closely the appearance of the newspapers your prospective printer already produces. Are the halftones sharp? Are they too dark or too light? Is the inking even throughout the paper? Are letters blurred or broken? Are the papers speckled with spots and lines where the printer has been careless about opaquing flaws in the negatives? Are the margins properly aligned? Is the paper folded evenly and without creases? Your paper will be judged by its looks as well as by its content, so beware of sacrificing printing quality for a slightly lower printing cost.

Schedule. Find out what day of the week he can print your paper, and how long it will take him to do it. The printer should easily be able to make the negatives and plates, prepare the press, and print all in one day. But he's likely to have a tight schedule during the week, with different newspapers being printed every day. You'll have to coordinate your own advertising and editorial deadlines with his available press time so that you can be sure of getting camera-ready pages to him at the same time every week.

Other services. Many newspaper printers also provide addressing, sorting, and mailing services, as well as pickup and delivery. You may find that at the outset these tasks, however tedious, can be accomplished by yourself and your staff more economically and with fewer mistakes; but it is useful to get bids for these services.

Cost. Most important, of course, is to find out how much the job will cost. Some newspaper printers have a standard price schedule, while others contract separately with each new customer. A typical standard price schedule includes a base price for printing the first 1,000 copies of an issue with a particular number of pages, and an additional lower charge for each additional 1,000 copies. Keep in mind that prices may vary significantly from one area to another.

Here is the price schedule (1983) of a relatively small circulation New England daily newspaper that also employs its press to print quite a number of other weekly and monthly papers:

16 pages, compact size:	first 1,000	$321.64
	each additional 1,000	38.95
24 pages, compact size:	first 1,000	450.96
	each additional 1,000	58.42
32 pages, compact size:	first 1,000	581.28
	each additional 1,000	77.90

The above prices do not include any extra camera work. This printer charges an additional $2.50 for each halftone or other photostat that must be made. The charge for using a second color on four pages, typically the front and back pages and the centerfold, is $60.

Another New England newspaper printer quoted the following prices for runs of 2,000, 3,000, 4,000, and 5,000 copies:

	2,000 copies	*3,000 copies*	*4,000 copies*	*5,000 copies*
16 pages	$300	$345	$385	$435
24 pages	435	490	540	600
32 pages	550	620	700	770

These charges include one halftone per page. Use of a second color on four pages costs $80.

Price guarantees. Finally, once you've found a printer who quotes a reasonable price and with whom you feel you can get along, it's a good idea to pin him down if you can to an agreement that he will not raise his price for a certain specified period, say, a year or more. A customary exception to this provision, however, permits the printer to change his price as the cost of paper changes; in recent years paper prices have consistently and sometimes dramatically increased.

Your printer is going to spend more time making negatives and plates and getting the press set up than he does actually running the press. Many web presses, once set up and operating smoothly, can produce 10,000 to 15,000 copies of a newspaper each hour. Leon used to complain that just when he got the bugs worked out and the press operating the way he wanted it to, he was all finished with our modest press run of 1,600. Other, less amiable printers may be reluctant to take on a paper that has a short press run; but keep searching until you find one who will charge you only for what you need.

You'll be dealing with your printer week in and week out, so plan to pay him regularly. It's customary in the newspaper printing trade to pay each week for the paper that was printed the previous week. At the same time, make sure you're getting what you pay for. Spend a day at the shop as your paper is being produced. Seeing and understanding the steps involved should give you some ideas that will save time, money, and headaches for you and the printer. Complain, though, if the inking is uneven or blurred, if good-quality photographs aren't reproduced well, or if the paper is cut or folded sloppily.

In fact, for the first dozen or so times you use the printer, until you have developed a solid sense of his expertise and concern for quality, it would be best if you could actually be present as the presses roll. Before a hundred papers come off the line you should have gone down the following checklist—and if anything is unacceptable, you should insist that the press be stopped and the error corrected:

► All pictures properly placed and right side up? (Watch those pesky real-estate ads with nearly identical houses; and watch any pictures with legible writing in them, such as signs, because the negative may have been flipped to the wrong side making the print appear backwards.)

► Picture reproduction good, not muddy or too light? (Initial inking as the press gets started is always uneven—these first copies should be discarded and the count started when quality is acceptable.)

► Inking of pages even?

► Pages imposed correctly, lined up at the top and with proper margins at right, left, top, bottom, and gutter?

► No black or white blots on pages?

► No streaking caused by defective press blanket?

► Trimming neat and properly positioned?

A. J. Liebling, who for many years wrote critically about American newspapers in the New Yorker, once commented that "freedom of the press is guaranteed only to those who own one." As publisher of a small newspaper you aren't likely to end up owning a printing press; but once you have a machine for setting type, master pasteup techniques, and find a cooperative printer, you'll be well on your way to journalistic independence.

5 Typography

TYPOGRAPHY IS THE PROCESS by which you produce the copy—the words and sentences that go into articles, headlines, and advertisements—for your newspaper. When most newspapers were printed by letterpress, metal type was set into lines, either by hand or by a Linotype machine, and used to make a direct impression on paper. This kind of typography is often called *hot type*, because the Linotype machine casts each line out of a molten lead alloy; it is still used by a very small (and ever dwindling) number of newspapers that continue to maintain their own hot-metal typesetting and letterpress printing shops.

A revolution has overtaken the newspaper industry in the last decades. It was precipitated by the advent of offset lithography, the printing process (described in the preceding chapter) that eliminates the need for hot-metal composition. With offset printing, all that is needed is a clear, sharp image of the copy to be reproduced; this image is then photographed, and the printing plate is made from the negative. Acceptably sharp copy can be produced on a good typewriter—such as the IBM Executive or Selectric—or on a more sophisticated kind of direct impression typesetter such as the IBM Selectric Composer or the Addressograph Multigraph Varityper. One could also use the output of a so-called letter-quality printer attached to a word processor, and thus take advantage of the word processor's text editing capacity in preparing copy.

But no direct impression or "strike-on" typesetting machine can equal the performance of *photocomposition* equipment for the production of *cold type,* that is, copy set not in metal lines of type but simply on paper. In most phototypesetting machines, the individual characters exist in negative form on a master filmstrip, grid, or disk, usually made of plastic or glass. An intense light is flashed through this master, and the characters are projected in rapid succession onto photographic paper, which is then developed. The copy thus produced is sharper and more regular than that of any machine that works according to the basic principles of the typewriter. Furthermore, it is possible to obtain photocomposition equipment that is relatively inexpensive, reliable, and remarkably versatile.

In writing this book we are assuming that you want to produce a newspaper in the most economical way; but we also assume that you want the best-looking and most professional result for your money and effort. To us this means setting your own type on equipment that you have either rented or purchased. It is not necessary to set your own type; you can prepare all of your edited copy and send it out to a commercial type house to be set—but to do that you'll need plenty of money. It can cost from $30 to $100 or more to buy type to fill an average compact-format newspaper page—that is, at least $480 for a sixteen-page newspaper, just for the typesetting—and what you get will not always be of very high quality. Moreover, you will be dependent on someone else's work schedule, with all the unforeseen delays and failures that implies.

However you get your type set, the most telling sign of the system's efficiency is the number of typographical errors in the copy. Careful proofreading is essential, of course; but proofreading is invariably done at the last minute, which means that some of the mistakes will get past you. And the more errors there are, the more corrections you'll have to set and paste in as the deadline hour approaches. All of this is time-consuming and nerve-racking, and is likely to give your newspaper a crooked, patchy appearance as well.

The ideal to strive for, then, is completely error-free copy. And it is possible to approach this ideal, even without a flawless typist—if you use phototypesetting equipment. These machines allow you to correct errors before they are actually set into type, because the characters are not projected onto the photographic paper at the same time they are entered on the keyboard but are held instead in the machine's memory. The simplest kinds of phototypesetters remember only one line of type at a time, so that you must catch your errors before the machine moves on to the next line. More sophisticated models have all the text editing capabilities of the best word processors, with built-in memories of thousands of characters and the ability to store copy on disks for subsequent editing, proofreading, and resetting if necessary. These machines make it possible to produce virtually perfect copy, and can save hours of pasteup work.

But there are other more important reasons for setting up your own in-house typesetting operation. There is no substitute for having a knowledgeable copy editor at the keyboard of the typesetter. No matter how carefully the copy is prepared, there will always be questions that arise as the type is being set. Is that the way Mrs. Thompson spells her first name? Was the new junior high school really built in 1962? Phototypesetting and word processing technology have made it possible to combine the editing and typesetting operations of the newspaper for a dramatic overall saving of time and labor. And new developments in this technology are taking place so rapidly that we are likely to see another whole revolution in publishing and communications within just a few years.

Modern typesetting machines are easy to use, clean, and small enough to fit comfortably in your home or office. We strongly recommend getting your own machine, unless you plan to publish so infrequently that it is uneconomical to do so. We set the type for the first three issues of the Harvard Post by renting time on an IBM Composer that was an hour's drive away—and it was murder. Even if you are able to rent time on someone else's machine at a good price, later, at layout time, you'll start tearing your hair as you discover that you forgot to set enough dates for all the pages, or that in setting a correction you made *another* mistake, or that you simply don't have enough copy to fill up the paper. If you are serious about putting out a good publication, you must have your own typesetting equipment, even if it is only an IBM typewriter to start with.

BASIC PRINCIPLES OF TYPOGRAPHY

Proportional spacing and justification. There is a fundamental difference between type that is "set" and that which is produced by an ordinary typewriter: each character, punctuation mark, and space on a typewriter takes up the same amount of horizontal space in a line. (The IBM Executive typewriter is an exception.) A lower-case *i* fills up the same space as does a capital *M*. But with hot-metal type, and any other kind of type that is designed to resemble hot metal, the horizontal space allotted to each character varies. This is called *proportional spacing,* and it gives to typeset copy a balance and visual gracefulness that makes it much more pleasing to the eye.

Another significant feature of the composing machine, as opposed to the typewriter, is that it can produce *justified* copy—columns of type in which the right-hand margin is vertically aligned, just as the left-hand margin is. Justification is accomplished by varying the *word spacing*—the amount of space between the words—from line to line. Almost all type-setting machines are able to do this automatically.

Typeset copy that is not justified is said to be set "ragged." A column of type that is aligned only on the left side has been set "ragged right," or "flush left," or "neat left." Conversely, if it is aligned only on the right side it is "ragged left," or "flush right," or "neat right." A third possibility is for each line to be centered, in which case the copy is ragged left and right.

There is a trend away from justification in modern composition. More and more books, magazines, and newspapers are set ragged right these days, at least in part. In deciding whether to justify your copy you should consider the kind of machine you are using, the design of your newspaper, and your own personal taste. Certain kinds of machines require that you type copy twice to justify it. With such machines it's best to leave it ragged. In general, the wider the column the worse it looks when set ragged, though there are exceptions.

But the walking of which I speak has nothing in it akin to taking exercise, as it is called, as the sick take medicine at stated hours—as the swinging of dumb-bells or chairs; but is itself the enterprise and adventure of the day. If you would get exercise, go in search of the springs of life. Think of a man's swinging dumb-bells for his health, when those springs are bubbling up in far-off pastures unsought by him!

Moreover, you must walk like a camel, which is said to be the only beast which ruminates when walking. When a traveller asked Wordsworth's servant to show him her master's study, she answered, "Here is his library, but his study is out of doors."

Living much out of doors, in the sun and wind, will no doubt produce a certain roughness of character—will cause a thicker cuticle to grow over some of the finer qualities of our nature, as on the face and hands, or as severe manual labor robs the hands of some of their delicacy of touch.

Justified copy set on a 13-pica column.

But the walking of which I speak has nothing in it akin to taking exercise, as it is called, as the sick take medicine at stated hours—as the swinging of dumb-bells or chairs; but is itself the enterprise and adventure of the day. If you would get exercise, go in search of the springs of life. Think of a man's swinging dumb-bells for his health, when those springs are bubbling up in far-off pastures unsought by him!

Moreover, you must walk like a camel, which is said to be the only beast which ruminates when walking. When a traveller asked Wordsworth's servant to show him her master's study, she answered, "Here is his library, but his study is out of doors."

Living much out of doors, in the sun and wind, will no doubt produce a certain roughness of character—will cause a thicker cuticle to grow over some of the finer qualities of our nature, as on the face and hands, or as severe manual labor robs the hands of some of their delicacy of touch.

Unjustified copy on the same measure.

Measuring type. Typographers use a system of measurement whose basic units are *points* and *picas*. For all practical purposes, there are six picas to an inch (in fact, a pica is very slightly less than one-sixth of an inch) and twelve points to a pica. Thus, there are 72 points to the inch. Newspaper column widths are measured in picas; most columns in the Harvard Post are 13½

8-point English Times
10-point Paladium
12-point Oracle
14-point Stymie
18-point Korinna
24-PT. COPPERPLATE
30-pt. Goudy Handtooled

---

picas, or 2¼ inches, wide. The different sizes of type are measured in points; for example, 8-point English Times, 10-point Paladium, or 12-point Oracle. The point size of the type does not refer to the height of any one character, but should be thought of in terms of the metal slugs used in hot-metal composition. Each such slug in any one size of type consists of a rectangular background piece of metal with a raised character on it. Even though the various characters in the alphabet are of different heights, all of the rectangular slugs are of the same height, and each one allows for a sufficient amount of space above and below the letters so that when they are set into lines the *ascenders* (the upper parts of the tall letters) and the *descenders* (the letters that extend below the baseline—*g, j, p, q,* and *y*) do not run into each other. It is the height of these slugs, in points, that is the size of the type; and the same system of measurement is carried over into cold type even though the slugs no longer exist.

Nine-point type therefore takes up a minimum of 9 points of vertical space per line. In actual practice, type is almost always set with some additional space, called *leading* ("ledding"), inserted between the lines. Nine-point type that is set with one point of extra leading between each line is said to be set "nine on ten." Ten-point type set with 2 points of leading is "ten on twelve," and so on. If no leading is used, the copy is said to be set "solid." The proper amount of leading is essential for the type to be readable; even one point of extra space (1/72 of an inch) makes an enormous difference in the way a column of type looks. In general, the wider the column, and the larger the size of the type itself, the more leading should be used—although the actual amount of leading will depend partly on the type style. (See example on following page.)

Another useful unit of typographic measurement is the *em*. The em is not a universal constant, but varies according to the size of the type being used: it is an area equal to the square of the size of the type. Thus, in 10-point type, an em space is 10 points high and 10 points wide. The term

Leaving the Nashua, we changed our route a little, and arrived at Stillriver Village, in the western part of Harvard, just as the sun was setting. From this place, which lies to the northward, upon the western slope of the same range of hills on which we had spent the noon before, in the adjacent town, the prospect is beautiful, and the grandeur of the mountain outlines unsurpassed. There was such a repose and quiet here at this hour, as if the very hill-sides were enjoying the scene, and we passed slowly along, looking back over the country we had traversed, and listening to the evening song of the robin, we could not help contrasting the equanimity of nature with the bustle and impatience of man.

Leaving the Nashua, we changed our route a little, and arrived at Stillriver Village, in the western part of Harvard, just as the sun was setting. From this place, which lies to the northward, upon the western slope of the same range of hills on which we had spent the noon before, in the adjacent town, the prospect is beautiful, and the grandeur of the mountain outlines unsurpassed. There was such a repose and quiet here at this hour, as if the very hill-sides were enjoying the scene, and we passed slowly along, looking back over the country we had traversed, and listening to the evening song of the robin, we could not help contrasting the equanimity of nature with the bustle and impatience of man.

Leaving the Nashua, we changed our route a little, and arrived at Stillriver Village, in the western part of Harvard, just as the sun was setting. From this place, which lies to the northward, upon the western slope of the same range of hills on which we had spent the noon before, in the adjacent town, the prospect is beautiful, and the grandeur of the mountain outlines unsurpassed. There was such a repose and quiet here at this hour, as if the very hillsides were enjoying the scene, and we passed slowly along, looking back over the country we had traversed, and listening to the evening song of the robin, we could not help contrasting the equanimity of nature with the bustle and impatience of man.

At top left, 9-point type is set "solid," with no additional leading between the lines. The same copy is set 9 on 10 at top right. Note the difference in readability. At bottom, on a wider measure, the same copy is set 10 on 12. In general, wider columns call for larger type and more leading for ease of reading.

"em" is sometimes mistakenly used interchangeably with "pica"; but the pica is always 12 points, whereas the em is 12 points wide only in 12-point type. The *en* is another unit of area measurement; its width is about half that of the em, while its height is the same. Thus, an en space in 10-point type is 10 points high and about 5 points wide.

The em and the en are most commonly used in referring to the widths of spaces and of certain punctuation marks and other characters. It is important, for instance, to distinguish among the *hyphen,* which is the very short dash used to break words at the ends of lines and to separate the parts of compound words such as "twenty-one" and "cul-de-sac"; the *en dash,* wider than the hyphen, and used to convey the sense of "to," or "from one to the other," as in "open Monday–Friday"; and the *em dash,* twice as wide as the en dash, and used to indicate a pause—like this. There is also, for example, the *en bullet,* a heavy black dot (•) taking up the space of an en and used to set off and draw attention to the material that follows it.

Distinguishing type styles. Most newspapers use 9- or 10-point type for their regular body copy. Some of the fancier kinds of typesetting machines produce type in half-point increments, making 9½-point body type another option. But even among the various kinds of 9-point type there are great variations in size, appearance, and readability. This is because of the tremendous variety of type styles that are available. Learning to distinguish among different type styles and to use them to the best advantage in your newspaper takes time and experience. But there are certain general principles that can be outlined here.

This is an example of 9-point Times Roman type.
This is an example of 9-point Century Light type.
This is an example of 9-point Futura Book type.
This is an example of 9-point Oracle (or Optima) type.

Most modern typefaces can be classified according to whether they employ *serifs,* the little finishing strokes that adorn the corners and extremities of the characters. Serif typefaces tend to look more traditional than *sans-serif* styles, those without serifs, which often appear more sleek and modern. Serif typefaces are more appropriate for the news and editorial copy in a newspaper; sans-serif styles, as well as the more ornamented serif styles, should be reserved for advertising and display uses.

This is a type style with serifs.
This is a sans-serif type style.

The names by which different type families are known—such as Times Roman, Bodoni, Baskerville, Caslon, Futura, Garamond—refer to an overall style that includes a variety of different faces. Within each family there can be variations in the weight, width, and angle of the characters. The weight refers to the thickness of the individual strokes. Any one type style may be available in several weights, designated by names such as light, medium, demibold, bold, extra bold, heavy, and black. The width of a typeface can be varied by compressing or expanding the characters horizontally without affecting their height: 11-point Univers Condensed type thus takes up less horizontal space than does regular 11-point Univers, even though they are identical in height. Similarly, 11-point Univers Extended takes up more space. The angle of the type may be either straight up and down, known as roman, or *slanted to the right, called italic.*

This is an example of a roman type in medium weight.
This is an example of medium italic type.
This is an example of a boldface type.
This is an example of bold italic type.
This is an example of bold condensed type.
This is an example of bold condensed italic type.
THIS EXAMPLE IS SET IN SMALL CAPITALS.

A complete set of typographic characters in any one family and in a particular size and weight is called a *font.* Thus, Souvenir is the name of a type family, or style; Souvenir Light is the name of a typeface; and 12-point Souvenir Light is the name of a font. A complete font contains all the letters, upper- and lower-case; the ten numerals; the various punctuation marks; and a variety of other characters ($¢*&/ + = †§@ ★ ✔#® •□©%) that are commonly used in setting type.

Choosing fonts for your paper. In choosing the type fonts that you will use in your newspaper it is best to start with a few standard styles and sizes that will serve a variety of purposes. Depending on the kind of machine you get, each new font can cost a considerable amount; it's best to avoid very

ABCDEFGHIJKLMNOPQRSTUVWXYZ&
abcdefghijklmnopqrstuvwxyz 1234567890

ABCDEFGHIJKLMNOPQRSTUVWXYZ&
abcdefghijklmnopqrstuvwxyz   1234567890

ABCDEFGHIJKLMNOPQRSTUVWXYZ&
abcdefghijklmnopqrstuvwxyz   1234567890

Three examples of 10-point Univers type: at top, 10-point Univers Condensed; below it, regular 10-point Univers; and, at bottom, 10-point Univers Extended. Note that the height of the characters remains constant.

decorative or bizarre typefaces that you will end up using only rarely. Your main text type should be chosen with great care. It should be compact and easy to read; the thickness of the strokes in the characters should not vary too much, or else the thin strokes will disappear altogether in the plate-making process or when the inking of the newspaper is not heavy enough. Your text type should be neither too light nor too bold; it should be free of annoying idiosyncrasies that might distract the eye of the reader.

Let's say you choose a 9-point type for your body copy; you will also want an italic or bold face (and preferably both) in the same style and size for giving emphasis to special words and sentences, and for setting captions and subheads. It is also useful to have at least one or two additional fonts in the same style as your main text font but in different sizes. A 7- or 8-point font, for example, would be good for setting classified ads; and 11- or 12-point could be used for folios (page numbers), headings, and titles. Sticking to the same style for several editorial design applications lends a sense of typographic unity to the newspaper. You will also need at least two or three fonts in contrasting styles for advertising copy. Four or five fonts in all will be enough to get you going; as you work from week to week you will soon discover which new sizes and styles would make the best additions to your type library. Deciding to buy a new font and poring over the catalogues to choose the right one is one of the special pleasures of the newspaper trade.

Display type. Whatever kind of typesetting machine you use, you will have to have some way of setting display type for headlines and advertisements. The best solution is to get equipment that can produce its own enlarged type. The CompuWriters—the very popular line of inexpensive phototype-setters made by the Compugraphic Corporation in the 1970s—can set type as large as 24-point, which is sufficient for most small-newspaper uses. The more expensive models of CompuWriters—the IV, 48, and 88—go up as far as 48-point or even 72-point type. The Harvard Post currently uses a Compugraphic EditWriter; this machine is available in two versions with the ability to set type as large as 36-point or 72-point, depending on which model you get. When we need type larger than our machine can produce, we either enlarge the copy on our photostat camera (see page 39) or use transfer lettering, such as Letraset (see page 94).

If you are setting copy on a typewriter or any other machine that can't give you enlarged type, you have four choices for getting display type. You can job it out to a commercial type house, which is expensive, time-consuming, and not recommended; you can buy a special headline-setting machine, which is also expensive and often troublesome; you can set the display copy on your typewriter or strike-on typesetter and then take it to someone who has a copy camera for photographic enlargement; or you can find someone nearby with typesetting equipment capable of producing display type and talk her into letting you use it. Most print shops, type houses, and commercial art and advertising agencies—as well as news-papers—have their own typesetting systems. Try to make friends with someone who works in such an office and will teach you how to operate the machine some evening or weekend.

Whichever of these methods you use, you will have to leave the headlines for the very end of your pasteup process to avoid disastrous last-minute changes and omissions. Transfer lettering is useful as a last resort in such situations, but don't expect to produce all of your display type that way. It is much too slow.

CHOOSING A TYPESETTING SYSTEM

A chaotic industry. The manufacture and sale of computerized typesetting equipment is an industry in the throes of rapid and continuous change. Six years ago, when we wrote the first edition of this book, the Compugraphic Corporation, based in Wilmington, Massachusetts, was the undisputed leader in the field of low-cost phototypesetters. One could buy a new CompuWriter for about $6,000, or $150 per month, and set up a type shop that would serve the small newspaper well. Compugraphic had just intro-duced the EditWriter, which, with its $16,000 price tag, became the most popular and successful typesetter ever built. Soon afterward, the company announced that it would no longer make CompuWriters, thereby effectively abandoning the huge market in inexpensive machines that Compugraphic alone had been serving. The EditWriter, though prohibitively expensive for some people, was also ideally suited to the small newspaper operation. Yet it, too, has now been discontinued by the manufacturer in favor of a new generation of machines—the Modular Composition System, or MCS.

In spite of significant advances in technology, the phototypesetting choices available to the buyer with limited resources are in many ways less satisfactory in 1983 than they were in 1977. It is impossible to buy any new equipment for less than $13,000, and it is not at all clear that what you can get at that price is worth having. There is a vigorous market in used machines, some selling for as little as $1,500, but shopping for an old type-setter is like buying a used car: risky. Reliable service is expensive and hard to find; frequent breakdowns are the small newspaper publisher's night-mare (we don't know anyone who runs a typesetting machine and has not at some time or other been reduced to tears by it); and Compugraphic won't say how long it will continue to support its old, discontinued models with service and spare parts.

Nevertheless, a slew of small companies have been springing up and trying to fill the breach left by Compugraphic's schizophrenic retreat from the low-cost typesetting market. A few reputable used equipment dealers, who sell and also service the machinery, have appeared. High-tech entrepreneurs are trying to bridge the gap between the old CompuWriters and the microcomputer explosion by marketing interfaces that can link the two devices, thus breathing new life into those "obsolete" typesetters. New developments are taking place virtually every week in typesetting and word processing technology that will surely create unpredictable pressures and possibilities.

Where does that leave you, the bewildered newcomer? We are reluctant to make specific recommendations here on what to buy, because by the time you read them they will probably be wrong. The advantages and disadvantages of the machines we have used are discussed below. Beyond that, there is some general advice that is sure to retain its value no matter what else changes:

¶ Get in touch with the major manufacturers of phototypesetting equipment to find out what they are currently making and how much it costs. Besides Compugraphic, they are: Itek Composition Systems, based in Rochester, New York; the Varityper Division of Addressograph Multigraph, based in Hanover, New Jersey; Mergenthaler Linotype Company, based in Plainview, New York; and Alphatype Corporation, based in Skokie, Illinois.

¶ Talk to everyone you can find in the typesetting or publishing business about the equipment they are using, have used, and are thinking of getting next.

¶ Check the telephone directory for used equipment dealers and independent repair services. Get recommendations from them on what to buy. If there aren't any in your area, try calling the Graphic Systems Exchange in Penfield, New York.

¶ Get a subscription to TypeWorld, the trade newspaper of the typesetting and word processing industry, by writing to Sam Blum, the publisher, at 15 Oakridge Circle, Wilmington, Mass. 01887. If you are a newspaper publisher, he'll put you on his mailing list at no charge.

¶ Before you buy anything—particularly used equipment or new machinery that hasn't been on the market very long—insist on seeing it in operation and confirming that it can actually do what you expect it to.

The IBM typewriter. If you are considering a very small-scale publishing enterprise and you have absolutely no money to start out with, you may want to try setting your copy on a typewriter. The IBM, with its unusually even striking impression and with the blackness of the characters it can produce with a carbon film ribbon, is one of the few kinds of typewriter that can generate acceptable copy for offset reproduction. There are other brands that have capabilities similar to the IBM's; we have never found one that held up as well with heavy use over time, or that was supported by such an excellent service and repair system. Moreover, the newer IBM models with their built-in correcting keys make typing much faster and more enjoyable.

The IBM Selectric typewriter uses a small, movable metal ball—often called a "golf ball"—instead of the traditional type bars. The golf ball whirls around and moves back and forth across the paper while the platen remains stationary. The balls are interchangeable and come in a variety of styles, enabling the Selectric to produce both roman and italic type. Some IBM typewriters employ a system of modified proportional spacing, which makes the type considerably more attractive than that produced by a conventional typewriter. Many small, cheaply produced newsletters are set on IBM typewriters, with good results.

IBM typewriter type should not be reproduced full-size for newspaper use. It will look much better on the page if your printer photographically reduces it to about 80 percent of its original size. You can simply type your copy and lay out complete pages that are 125 percent as large, in every dimension, as you want the finished pages to be. If the finished page is to be 10 inches wide and 14 inches deep, for instance, the layout you give the printer should be 12½ inches wide and 17½ inches deep—with the instruction to shoot it at 80 percent. (If you do this, be sure to compensate for the reduction when you calculate the reproduction size of halftones; see *Pasteup,* pages 97–98.)

It is possible to justify your copy on an IBM typewriter; the procedure is described in the machine's operating manual, or see Clifford Burke's description of it in his book *Printing It.* It involves typing the material twice; considering the time consumed and the appearance of the finished product, it is simply not worth the effort.

New IBM typewriters (in 1983) cost between $900 and $2,000. It is possible to find a good used one if you shop around, but expect to pay at least $500 to get one in good condition. It is also possible to rent or lease typewriters directly from IBM or from local office machine dealers. A lease usually lets you build up equity towards eventual purchase of the machine, whereas a rental does not. If you lease or rent a typewriter from IBM, the company assumes responsibility for keeping it in good working order.

The IBM Composer. The Composer was IBM's attempt to make a fancy typewriter that approximated some of the capabilities of a real typesetting machine, including a true proportional spacing system and a wide selection of interchangeable type balls that let you produce a number of classic typefaces in sizes from 6- to 12-point. It is easy to use and, unlike a photo-typesetter, requires few expensive accessories. It comes in two versions, the regular Composer and the Electronic Selectric Composer, or ESC.

A major problem with the standard Composer is figuring out how to handle typographical errors, as the machine has no memory and no correcting feature. This means that you have to waste time with correcting tape or fluid, or just pasting in endless corrections. The ESC has a memory, of sorts. When you make an error you can back up, type in the correction, and then get the correct copy when the machine later spits out the type. But you still have to use some sort of "white-out" or other cover-up, or else your original copy will be a mess, full of superimposed characters, and you won't be able to tell, when you look back over it, what you've actually got in the machine's memory.

The IBM Composer might be a useful machine for producing a small newsletter, but it is not recommended for newspaper work.

Phototypesetting. Whereas the Composer is essentially a sophisticated cousin of the typewriter, the phototypesetting machine is an entirely different beast. There are hundreds of different kinds of phototypesetters, but all of them work by either a *photomechanical* or a *digitized* process. The photomechanical variety, which are generally less expensive, work like this:

The type font is not a metal ball or a set of bars that strikes against paper but an opaque plastic filmstrip or glass disk on which the characters appear in transparency. Film fonts are usually affixed to the outside of a cylindrical drum, which spins rapidly inside the machine when it is running, causing the characters to pass in front of a bright stroboscopic light. The operator of the machine types the copy on a typewriter-like keyboard. The machine's computer causes the strobe light to flash at exactly the right instants to project the proper characters from the film through a lens, which is mounted on a carriage or turret in front of the spinning drum. The characters are projected in precise alignment onto a roll of photographic paper. This whole process takes place inside the closed machine in complete darkness—it is, in effect, its own darkroom. The exposed paper is fed into a light-tight container, or cassette, which is later removed from the machine. The paper is then developed in a stabilization processor and, after drying, is ready for pasteup.

Digitized typesetting is, according to the experts, the wave of the future. It eliminates the film master, the strobe light, and the lens—all

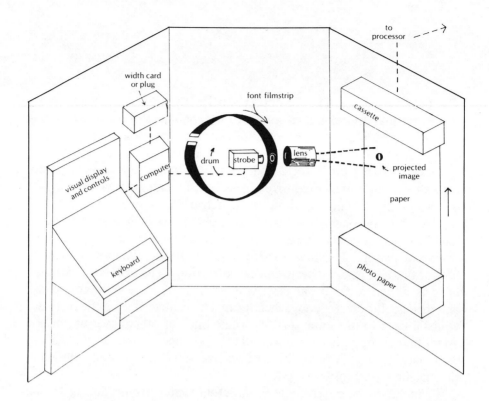

The phototypesetting process.

elements of the photomechanical process that are especially subject to damage and wear. Digitized typographic characters are formed on a cathode-ray tube (CRT) by means of an extremely high resolution matrix, or grid of minute points of light, and are stored on a disk, like any other electronic information, instead of on a plastic or glass negative. The type is transferred directly from the CRT screen to the photographic paper. This process is considerably faster than photomechanical typesetting. At this writing, digitized typesetters are much more expensive than other varieties.

Phototypesetting produces very sharp, clear copy; in some ways it is even better looking than traditional hot type, because the image that is obtained through these photographic and chemical means is not subject to the variations of quality caused by imperfections and wear in metal. Furthermore, the computer is able to accomplish a variety of typesetting functions—particularly justification—with great ease.

Controls on the typesetter allow you to tell the computer how long each line of type is to be, how much leading to use, and the minimum and maximum amounts of space that are to be allowed between words. The computer decides where to end each line, so that the word spaces will be within the limits you have set. The machine can also center material easily, or position it flush right or flush left.

Some typesetters are equipped with automatic hyphenation programs that decide where to break words at the ends of lines. We don't like them, because we've never seen one that didn't make horrendous mistakes. English syllabification and pronunciation are illogical, and that means that the person at the keyboard, not the computer, should decide where to put the hyphens. Typographic engineers continue to search for the perfect computer hyphenation program, because they cannot tolerate the thought that truth might be ultimately illogical.

The CompuWriters. Compugraphic sold about 20,000 of these machines in various versions before halting production of them, and almost all of them are still out there in small newspaper and type shops, beeping and whirring along as they grow older and their worried owners try to figure out how to keep them alive for another few years. The Harvard Post's first photo-typesetter, a CompuWriter I named Typo, is now eight years old and still going strong, although most of our typesetting is now done on our EditWriter, Ed.

The CompuWriters are basically good, reliable machines, with a few significant shortcomings. First, none is equipped with a disk storage capacity enabling you to capture keystrokes and hold them in the machine's memory, and the memory capacity itself is very small—only one line of type. Second, the CompuWriter's visual display is primitive and confusing,

The CompuWriter IV, which is similar in appearance to the other CompuWriters but has more controls on its keyboard.

unable, for example, to show lower-case letters. Third, the number of type fonts *on line* (that is, accessible through keystrokes rather than manual changing of fonts) is very small in the lower range of machines. Fourth, some models (the CompuWriter Junior and the CompuWriter II, Junior) are severely limited in the range of type styles they can accommodate. Fifth, all but the fanciest models lack a tabbing function, which makes the setting of multiple-column material difficult and time-consuming. Finally, obtaining service and spare parts for CompuWriters may become exceedingly difficult as the years pass.

In spite of these problems, people will undoubtedly continue to buy used CompuWriters—at least until someone comes along with a simple, serviceable typesetter that sells for under $10,000. What's more, several small companies are developing interfaces for connecting CompuWriters with word processors (see below), and even Compugraphic is planning to market a "front-end" system (keyboard, monitor, and computer) that can be plugged into the photo output unit of a CompuWriter IV. This last development is especially newsworthy, for it is the first time that Compugraphic has acknowledged that its old machines aren't hopelessly obsolete.

Used CompuWriters are selling for anything from $1,500 to $7,000 (in 1983). It would be well worth it to pay a premium to a reputable dealer who agrees to service the machine for you.

The CompuWriter and the word processor. Two of the main disadvantages of the CompuWriter—the lack of disk storage and machine memory and the primitive display unit—can be overcome by connecting the machine to a microcomputer equipped with a word processing program. This is done with an interface, a lump of electronic circuitry that translates information from the microcomputer's internal language into the CompuWriter's internal language. Such an arrangement theoretically gives you all the text editing and storage capabilities of the EditWriter; in practice, the value of the system will depend on the quality of the microcomputer and the software you are using.

The CompuWriter–interface–microcomputer system could be a very attractive alternative for the small newspaper publisher, especially if you already own one of the components. Even if you're starting from scratch, there are some distinct advantages to this system. For $10,000 or less, you can equip yourself with a fairly powerful typesetter—and at the same time acquire a computer that will greatly streamline your bookkeeping and business operations. (More on this subject is found in Chapter 10, *Financial Matters.*)

Several companies are manufacturing or developing interfaces for the CompuWriter. One of the oldest and most reputable is G.O. Graphics in

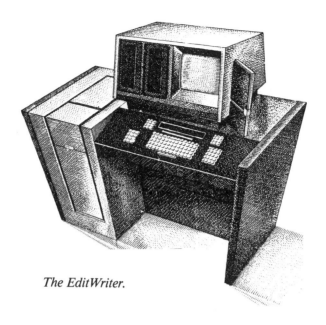

The EditWriter.

Lexington, Massachusetts. The 1983 price for their interface is $1,495; for an extra $200 you can get one with a modem (a telecommunications hook-up that enables your computer to talk to other computers by phone).

The EditWriter. Like the CompuWriter, the EditWriter is no longer manu-factured, but is destined to remain a workhorse of the small typesetting operation for many years. About 38,000 of them were sold, so the market in used machines and the chances for getting them properly serviced are likely to be good for quite some time.

The beauty of the EditWriter is that it is a very logical machine. The typographic, editing, and text storage commands that the user must learn are straightforward; and the screen monitor is well designed and easy to read. People *enjoy* using EditWriters—even people who don't otherwise trust computers and word processors. We taught a twelve-year-old friend of ours to use the machine; within a couple of hours she was setting type with the confidence of a professional.

The EditWriter is not without flaws. Its automatic hyphenation program is awful, and it doesn't warn you when a justified line of type has been set too "loose"—that is, with too much word spacing. It sets type in only twelve different sizes (plenty for a small newspaper), whereas similar machines—Addressograph Multigraph's Comp/Set and Comp/Edit, for instance—have a much wider range.

The EditWriter comes in a variety of models, each with its own special features and options. A good used equipment dealer will help explain these details. Compugraphic itself is still selling reconditioned EditWriters as of 1983. At this writing, used models cost from $8,000 to $15,000. Quality and prices vary widely; it pays to shop around.

Dark Horse

by *Edit Writer*

A NEW MEMBER OF THE STAFF

HI! Allow me to introduce myself. My name is Edit Writer 7500, but you can call me Ed. Miller, your regular columnist, is in a bad mood this week, so I'm taking over this spot.

I first came to work at THE HARVARD POST only a week ago, but already I can see that I'm going to like it here. In case you're wondering, I'm not actually a human being. I am a fabulously sophisticated COMPUTER PHOTOTYPESETTING MACHINE. I can do things that these mere people at the Post can't even imagine. And, believe me, there are going to be some big changes made around here. For one thing, I write the columns from now on. And I think there ought to be a regular feature called "Computers About Town." There's also going to be a new category in the classified ads for "Computer Time Sharing," and the page with news about PEOPLE and CLUBS is going to have to give equal space to FLOPPY DISKS.

Up till now, you see, the Post has been setting all its type on a ridiculously simple machine (a distant cousin of mine, actually, from a pitifully obsolete branch of the family). That useless piece of scrap iron can't even hyphenate w-ords by itself, like I can. And **get this:** it sets type in only *one size at a time,* and it can't mix different type styles on the same line!

You can hardly blame them, but the people here at the Post have a tendency to think small. They've been working with such limited equipment. But all that is over. From now on we **think big.** **We think bold** And we're going to give this newspaper some *class.*

Why should you have to stick to one lousy type style in a newspaper article? That's boring. People use lots of *different* styles in advertisements and it looks just fine. AND I THINK IT'S DUMB TO HAVE TO ALWAYS USE THE SAME SIZE TYPE. This isn't a funeral — *it's a newspaper.*

And I don't understand why all the lines have to be straight either. *Innovate!* That's my philosophy. DON'T LET THE !?&@#☆!✓¶◄►$ CRAMP YOUR STYLE.

Uh-oh. Here comes Miller to see what I've been up to. But it's all right. HE DOESN'T KNOW HOW TO WORK ME YET! **Nyah, nyah!**

I'll do what I want and you can't stop me. No matter what you do I'll be able to outsmart you

---

The Compugraphic salespeople maintain that the new MCS with its digitized type is a vast improvement over the EditWriter. We haven't had a chance to use an MCS yet. In any case, the cheapest digitized MCS costs about $30,000—a lot of money for a small newspaper publisher. There is a photomechanical version of the MCS that sells for as little as $13,000; Compugraphic doesn't like to talk about it, and it's not clear whether this system is a good buy. If you're considering one, talk first with somebody who's been using one for a while.

Papers, chemicals, and processors. Whatever kind of phototypesetting machinery you use, you will have to have a processor, or developer, to make use of what comes out of the typesetter. There are several kinds of processors on the market; your choice should depend on the kind of type-setting machine you have, the kind of photographic paper it uses, and the conditions under which you will be working.

Great strides have been made in the past few years in improving the quality of phototypesetting paper and processing. The goal is to produce a crisp, black image on a pure white background, and to get that image to be reasonably permanent. Many older typesetters are equipped to use a kind of paper called Grade "S." Our experience with this paper was very poor: we found that in hot and humid weather (our office was not air-conditioned) the type began to fade away very rapidly, sometimes in a matter of hours. We switched to a kind of paper called Durographic, with much improved results.

Grade S and Durographic paper work in much the same way. Each is made with a light-sensitive coating that contains a developer. The image of the type is exposed onto the paper inside the typesetter by the bright strobe light, and the paper is then run through a processor consisting of two chemical baths—an activator, which triggers the developing process, and a stabilizer, which stops it just a few moments later. There are several kinds of processor available that will adequately develop either kind of paper. The most popular is the CompuKwik, currently selling for about $1,100. Used processors can be found; be watchful, though, for worn rollers and gears.

Other kinds of papers and processors yield higher-quality and more permanent copy, but at a much greater cost. Among these alternatives are the Permagraphic paper and processor and the so-called RC, or resin-coated, papers. These are more closely related to the papers used for printing photographs; they are generally developed by means of a four-step process, including a developer bath, a stop bath, a fixing bath, and a final wash. RC processors usually cost $4,000 and up.

With any processor, a strict maintenance regimen is essential. Old chemicals should be drained from the machine and fresh ones put in at regular intervals—preferably every day. The entire processor should be taken apart and thoroughly cleaned once a week. Handle the rollers with special care. One nick or crack can ruin your copy, and necessitate an expensive replacement.

Service—the big headache. The worst thing about all phototypesetters is getting them fixed when they break down. This is partly because of the high cost and difficulty of finding an experienced, reliable repairer, and partly because the machine invariably breaks at the worst time—on deadline day. For these reasons it is essential that you have a back-up machine available. You needn't own it. Talk to other people who run typesetting operations in your area and try to set up reciprocal aid agreements under which each of you can use the other's machine in an emergency.

While you're at it, talk to other compositors about the service problems they've experienced—especially if they are using the same kind of machine you are. Get recommendations for independent local repair services, which are likely to be less expensive than using the services of the machine's manufacturer. Above all, learn to troubleshoot machine malfunctions on your own. Many problems can be traced to mechanical rather than electronic causes; you'll be surprised to find out how many malfunctions result from a loose screw, or a paper clip that has slipped down into the works, or a fingerprint on a filmstrip.

One good way to save money on repairs is to buy replacement parts from the original manufacturers. Most machine components are not made by the typesetting companies, who generally add outrageous mark-ups to the prices they pay to their suppliers. For example, we recently bought a new CRT monitor for our EditWriter. The part is made by GTE Sylvania, from whom we were able to get a replacement for $115. Compugraphic charges $432.51 for the exact same part—and that doesn't include installation.

An excellent publication for users of Compugraphic equipment is "Glitches," an independent newsletter put out by Maverick Publications, Drawer 5007, Bend, Oregon 97708. A ten-issue subscription costs $25. It contains a directory of independent Compugraphic service companies and a large section of ads for used equipment. The same company publishes separate newsletters for users of Addressograph Multigraph and Mergenthaler typesetting equipment.

SOME TIPS FOR THE TYPOGRAPHER

¶ The typographer should always have a good dictionary within arm's reach, and should not hesitate to check the meaning, spelling, and proper hyphenation of words. We use *The American Heritage Dictionary,* published by Houghton Mifflin. Its clearly written definitions, inclusion of many proper names and places, and helpful usage notes and lists of synonyms make it a pleasure to read. A half-minute taken now and then to look up a word may seem to slow down the typesetting process; ultimately, though, it saves time by avoiding the need for corrections, and it greatly improves the quality of a newspaper.

¶ Make a typographic style sheet on which you note all the measurements and constants that are used repeatedly in setting type. Be sure to note the widths of the various column sizes, along with the proper amounts of leading. Write down anything that you find yourself having to look up frequently.

¶ Establish an invariable routine for setting up the machine, and let this routine become second nature to you: for example, check paper, check width cards or plugs, change gears (if necessary), check lens selector, change filmstrips, set line length and other parameters, push "prime" button (on CompuWriters), and begin. This will minimize the chance of a foul-up.

¶ Study up on common typographic questions: learn to put commas and periods inside quotations marks, colons and semicolons outside; to use brackets instead of parentheses for editorial interjections inside quotations; to spell out numbers when they come at the beginning of a sentence; and so on.

¶ Tight word spacing is usually better than wide spacing in justified copy; a succession of widely spaced lines will result in "rivers" in the type—distracting paths of white space running down the page. Tight spacing can often be accomplished by hyphenating at the end of the line even though it is not entirely necessary.

¶ Be sure to read the remarks about hyphenation in the *Chicago Manual of Style.* Hyphenation should always follow pronunciation, and the dictionary should be consulted in doubtful cases. Never break a one-syllable word; never leave a single letter standing alone at the end or beginning of a line.

¶ Arrange your work to minimize the number of time-consuming machine adjustments. When you are setting ad copy, for example, group the type styles so that there are fewer font changes.

¶ In setting copy for ads, be sure to leave enough room for borders. If your columns are 14 picas wide, the copy for a one-column ad should be set on no more than a 13-pica measure.

¶ Leave extra space between words that are set all in capitals.

¶ Make an ellipsis (three dots . . .) with periods that have a little extra space inserted between them.

¶ Do not use too much leading between the lines of headlines and other display type. One or two extra points is almost always enough. Do leave extra space, though, when switching from one size or style of type to another in the next line.

¶ Headlines look best when they fill up as much of the available horizontal space as possible. They should never be wider than the body copy directly below, however.

¶ Paragraph indents should be one em space for narrow columns; one or two em spaces for wider columns.

¶ Don't work for too long without developing the copy; if something has gone wrong you'll save yourself extra resetting.

¶ Break yourself of the habit of spacing twice after periods, colons, or other punctuation. The typesetter justifies lines by ending them at the last word space, so if that space was preceded by another space the line will come out looking unjustified—it will have a space at the end.

¶ Learn to override the minimum word space limit in certain situations. Headlines, in particular, often look all right with the words pushed closer together than usual—especially if the words are capitalized.

¶ Learn to improvise characters that don't appear on your machine. For example, some keyboard layouts lack the en dash; it can be improvised by pushing two hyphens together. The "cents" symbol (¢) can be made by superimposing a lowercase *c* and a virgule (slash).

¶ Watch out for the "quad left" function; it generally causes a little extra space to be added at every stroke of the space bar in the line. Do not use it, therefore, when setting lists and other copy where vertical alignment is important.

¶ Learn to reduce the extra space that occurs between certain combinations of letters. This is called *kerning*. A few typesetters can do this automatically; most require the typographer to do it manually. In the example below, the second line has been kerned.

A VAT OF SALTWATER TAFFY
A VAT OF SALTWATER TAFFY

¶ Clean your filmstrips regularly with soft tissue and font cleaner. Handle the film only by the edges, and store it hanging up in a cool, dark place.

¶ Remember that the chemicals in your processor are affected by temperature. Avoid extremes. Note that a little of the activator mixed into the stabilizer does no harm, but even a tiny amount of stabilizer in the activator ruins it.

¶ Make sure that the paper is being fed into the cassette properly before you start setting type. Some cassettes have slots that are a bit too narrow, causing the paper to jam. If yours is this way, loosen the screws a little.

¶ Fold the corners of the exposed paper to form a point before feeding it into the processor. Otherwise it can get tangled up inside the works.

¶ When something goes wrong with your machine, stop and make your own investigation of the symptoms before calling the repair service. Figure out exactly what the machine is doing wrong, and when it does it.

¶ Learn how to analyze flaws in your copy and diagnose the trouble. Common culprits are light leaks, dirt on the filmstrip, foreign matter in the processor, old chemicals, using the wrong width card or plug, or having the filmstrip improperly affixed to the drum.

¶ The darkness of the copy can be adjusted on some machines by means of gelatin filters placed in front of the lens. If your copy is always too dark or too light, and the machine has no intensity adjustment, ask your supplier for a set of filters.

6 Design and Layout

THE DESIGN AND LAYOUT of your newspaper is one of the most creative stages of putting it together; its quality is just as important as the quality of the writing that goes into the paper. It is a continual challenge to solve the puzzle of Copy into Page in fresh and attractive ways—and the small-format newspaper has special problems to contend with, problems that cannot always be solved by reliance on the "rules" laid down for large-format papers.

The small-format newspaper's page size will be about 11 inches wide and anywhere from 14 to 17 inches deep. Side and head margins will reduce the actual type page by about half an inch on each side and one inch at top and bottom. Into this type area can be fit anywhere from two to six columns, ranging from 9 picas (1½ inches) up through 29 picas (4 5/6 inches) in width.

There are several factors to keep in mind when choosing the width for your newspaper's standard column. A good, flexible design must accommodate news copy, pictures, advertising, and at least one optional width for features or editorials. The size of the typeface you plan to use will also be a determining factor: if you set your type on an IBM typewriter, for example, you'll want wider columns than if you're planning to use 9-point phototype.

The most common column size used in small-format newspapers is 11 picas, making a five-column page with *gutters* of about 1½ picas between the columns. This width nicely matches that of the standard advertising column—used by almost all who professionally prepare advertising—which measures 10 to 11 picas wide. A five-column design offers a good deal of flexibility in layout, and it can save headaches and even increase revenues because of its conformity to standard ad widths. (See *Advertising,* pages 103–104.)

On the other hand, a 10- or 11-pica column is not always easiest on the reader's eye. Compositors have developed a formula for the *optimum line length,* that is, the column width that makes for the easiest reading, based on the size of the type. For 9-point type the optimum line length is about 14 picas; for 10-point type it is about 15½ picas. Four columns measuring 13½ picas will fit nicely into a small-format page, with gutters of slightly more than 2 picas. (Four 14-pica columns will also work, with gutters of about 1⅓ picas.) But a four-column page presents certain difficulties. It is less flexible with regard to placement of pictures, stories, and ads; you really have to work to avoid a squared-off, boxy appearance to the finished page. Advertising must either be prepared so that it fits agreeably into the wider columns, or be designed with a different column size and "squared off" in a rectangular block on the page so as not to interfere with the four-column editorial format. (See *Advertising,* page 103, for a discussion of how advertising rates are affected by the four-column page.)

A three-column page is commonly used by small-format papers, either as standard practice or as an alternative page design for a paper using narrower columns. To be read most easily, a three-column page (with, perhaps, 19-pica columns and 2-pica gutters) should be set in a slightly larger type and with slightly more leading between the lines. Papers using a three-column page often sell their advertising on the basis of a six-column page, with two columns of advertising corresponding to one column of news.

A two-column page, with each column about 29 picas wide, is hard to read unless the text type is really quite large. For some time the Harvard Post used this width on its editorial page; but we abandoned its boxy appearance for a more flexible design using two 21½-pica columns and one of our standard 13½-pica columns. Varying the size of columns within a single page like this creates special layout and copyfitting problems, but it can add an element of variety and interest to your standard design. For example, a five-column page design could be varied by using three standard columns and one double-width column of about 23½ picas.

It's a good idea to assign a standard column width to most of your news matter, and then to work out alternative widths that can be used for editorial page material, features, and the like. Once a modest variety of widths is established, it can be used to create a design for your paper that is attractively diverse, but that works toward an overall unity.

Four examples of different column widths. Top left, a three-column page. Top right, four columns. Bottom left, five columns. Bottom right, the rarely used six-column page; gutters between columns are so small that column rules are used.

Some newspapers use thin rules between their columns, which allows them to get away with less gutter space. It's a device that conveys an old-fashioned look; we prefer to use a little more space and no rules.

Don't be afraid of designing a good deal of white space into your newspaper page. Especially if you envision using rather large, bold display type, generous amounts of white space work effectively to make the paper easier to read. It is much better to use white space carefully on the page than to leave the eye nowhere to rest between the grey columns of type, headlines, and pictures.

Choosing a typeface to use in your newpaper is an important step. Most newspapers use the more traditional serif typefaces; in large type blocks they are easier to read than the unadorned sans-serif faces like Helvetica (also known as Helios) or Univers, which are commonly used in advertising and newsletters. Be sure to select a face that has little variation of thick and thin strokes—your offset printer's camera is all too likely to miss altogether the fine lines of a lovely face like Palatino (also called Paladium). The best choices are the classic Times Roman faces, or perhaps Century.

The size of your text type should depend in large part on the width of your columns. We use a 9-point type set on 9½ points of space with our standard four-column page. Study other newspapers to determine which size suits you best; but remember, the larger your typeface, the more leading you must allow.

The choice of a headline style is also an important one to the overall appearance of your paper. Whether your preference is for a bold, breezy look or for a more sober, traditional one, the headline style you choose will do a lot to determine it. Decide now whether you want each important word in your headlines to start with a capital letter, or whether you want to use the lower-case style except for proper nouns and the first word in the headline. More on headline design appears on pages 86–88 in this chapter.

Similarly, the display type you choose for your newspaper's name as it appears on the front page is an expression of your paper's personality. Choose the typeface for the nameplate with care, as you'll have to live with it a long time. There are many distinctive styles available—check a transfer lettering catalog—that might serve well for the nameplate; just make sure that both in size and spirit the type you choose reflects the way you want your newspaper to come across.

The Harvard Post

Vol. X, No. 463   Harvard, Massachusetts, Friday, April 1, 1983   Twenty-Five Cents

PROVINCETOWN ADVOCATE

Vol. CVI, No. 26, 25 Cents   The Outer Cape Newspaper for 105 Years   Thursday, August 21, 1975

THE SHETLAND TIMES

1975 — No. 38   REGISTERED AT THE POST OFFICE AS A NEWSPAPER   PRICE SIX PENCE   19th SEPTEMBER, 1975

Three nameplates.

CONSTANTS

Certain things in any good newspaper will remain constant from issue to issue; before you finish the design of your paper you will have given careful thought to each of these. Some pages will always be free of ads, for example; the front page and the editorial page are usually among them. Certain types of copy—news, features, opinion columns—will usually fit into a certain column size. And other continuing features will have identifying titles or logos in approximately the same place in each edition. Listed here are the constants that should appear in each issue of the newspaper.

The nameplate. Sometimes called the *flag* (and often mistakenly called the masthead), this is the name of the newspaper as it appears at the top of the front page. (See illustration.)

Front page folio lines. Under the nameplate in each issue of the newspaper the reader should be able to find the day and date of that edition, the volume number and issue number, the name of the place of publication if that is not contained in the name of the paper, the price of a single copy, and possibly the second-class mail indicia (which can go anywhere in the first five pages). All this information is often underscored by a horizontal rule across the page, or enclosed within two such rules.

Inside page folio lines. Every inside page must also have certain information on it, usually at the top of the page: the name of the newspaper (and place of publication if that's not in the name); the date (if it's a weekly, there's no need to repeat the day of the week); and the page number. This information can be strung out across the top of the page (the page number should go on the outside corner), or it can be run together and placed at the outside corner.

Masthead. The masthead is the box traditionally included on the editorial page of a newspaper in which the basic information about its ownership, staff, and publication is found. Among the information that should appear is:

¶ the name of the newspaper, preferably in a reduced size of the same type used on the front-page nameplate;

¶ the folio information—date, volume and issue numbers, and page number—which on the editorial page is traditionally not put in its usual top-of-page position;

¶ the place of publication, including a mailing address;

¶ the frequency and day or days of publication;

¶ copyright notice; we say "Copyright © 1983 [or whatever] by The Harvard Post. All rights reserved. No part of this publication may be reproduced by any means without the express permission of the publishers.";

¶ the name(s) of the publisher(s);

¶ the name(s) of the editor(s);

¶ the names and titles of other editors, reporters, advertising manager or representatives, bookkeeper, and so forth; we use a special category called "Contributors to This Issue" so that we don't have to regularly list occasional contributors who aren't on the permanent staff:

¶ subscription prices;

¶ advertising rates, or a note that such rates may be obtained by request;

¶ telephone number, office hours, and information on news and advertising deadlines.

Second-class mail indicia. If you mail the newspaper under a second-class permit, postal regulations require that somewhere in the first five pages, in a place easily found by the reader, you print the words "Second-class postage paid at (city), (state, zip code)." We print this on the masthead; it's also often put with the information near the front-page nameplate. (See pages 118–121 for more information on postal regulations.)

Special section headings. Certain regular pages in the newspaper—the editorial page, the sports page, the review page, the food page are just a few possibilities—will have their own special headings in a larger, distinctive type style. This gives a feeling of continuity to the newspaper from issue to issue; and if you stick to using one or two styles for these headings, it will add a unified look to the design of the paper as well.

Column headings. Any regular column, whether or not it appears without fail in every issue, deserves its own special heading and perhaps a small picture to serve as a logo. We give such headings to our regular opinion columns, our gardening column, our food column, and the like.

Once the task of designing the format of your paper has been completed, you will need to make up layout sheets for use in production. On large sheets of paper, draw the outline of the full type page and the edges of the standard columns to precise measure in black ink, and draw horizontal rules at intervals of one-half inch at most. (We use our typesetting machine to prepare these rules at 12-point intervals.) If you have a commonly used alternative column width, make separate sheets for each. Take these to your printer and have him or her print up a hefty supply of them on heavy white paper in nonreproducible ink. With the help of these layout sheets and a light table and T-square, you should be able to achieve straight copy with little trouble.

PREPARING THE ADS

Designing your ads and specifying type for advertising copy is at least as challenging and creative a task as designing the other elements in your newspaper. It's a job that requires a good knowledge of typography, a strong visual sense, and a great deal of ingenuity. It helps tremendously to have a competent and imaginative advertising representative who will have screened out impossible situations (see *Advertising,* page 112); in fact, it helps if the same person is able to do both jobs, but that's not always possible.

There are certain things to keep in mind as you're translating your ad representative's mock-ups into cold type to lay out into the ads your readers will see in the paper:

Limit your type styles. Figure out which of your available typefaces are best for advertising, and use them judiciously. By sticking to a limited number of styles—perhaps five or six—you make it easier on the typesetter and yourself, and you give your advertising a distinctive, simple look that both the reader and the advertiser will appreciate. A good rule of thumb is to use no more than three different type styles within any one ad. A small-format newspaper will not need to use advertising display type larger than about 30 points, so you ought to be able to set almost all the type on your own composition equipment. (If you have access to a photostat camera, you can enlarge type from your typesetting machine as well.) If you're new at specifying type, work with a sample sheet of your available typefaces at hand, so you don't get mixed up.

Make use of white space. An ad with too much fine print and no display type will look crowded; the same amount of small print will come off very well if you allow a certain amount of white space and display type (other than the name of the business) to provide relief for the eye.

Too many gimmicks spoil the ad at left and give it a cluttered, even tacky appearance. At right, a clean ad that makes a memorable point by an arresting use of display type and white space.

At left, a too-large, reversed ad dwarfs editorial copy and will cause smudging on other pages. Above, effective use of white space and artwork in a simply laid out ad.

Use pictures. Even a small picture will dress up a simple ad and increase its readership. It's better to use a picture and make the type smaller than to use large type with no visual relief. And make use of any artistic talent on the staff to fill in when commercial art clipping books (see pages 112–113) don't have the right illustration.

Decorative borders. A wide variety of decorative border tapes is available; but stick to half a dozen, so you won't end up with a confused look to your page. Avoid garish designs and heavy (more than 4 points) black rules. Don't waste your money on special-occasion border tapes (jingle bells and holly, for example); your big commercial art book will have enough to get you through the season.

Reversed ads. A reversed ad is one that is shot separately by the printer so that it comes out with white type on a black background. Watch out for reversed ads more than a quarter-page in size; they require heavy inking, which will adversely affect photographs printed on the same spread, and they get your readers' hands dirty. (Some newspapers charge extra for reversed ads to cover the printer's extra camera work; this will depend on whether your own printer charges you for it.) You can also insist on toning down reversed ads by having them screened to less than 100 percent black.

Specifying type. When you're ready to begin specifying type for the advertising copy, the way you proceed will depend on the typesetting system you are using. If it is an EditWriter, Comp/Set, CompuWriter IV, or other machine with a large variety of type sizes and styles on line, you will be able to set up entire ads in one typesetting operation. In this case, simply mark up the ad in a different color pencil for type style and sizes; the typographer can take it from there, and you will end up with a nearly finished ad requiring almost no pasteup alterations. This ease of ad preparation is one of the wonderful aspects of the EditWriter and similar systems.

If you must work with a more primitive typesetter, here is the procedure to use in specifying type. First, assemble several sheets of clean paper. Each will be headed with the name of a particular typeface and size ("20-point Souvenir Medium," for example) and divided into categories for one-column, two-column, three-column, and four-column ads, or whatever variety of ad widths you use. The typographer will be able to save you much cutting and pasting by setting the copy within the limits of the correct column width. (Note: ad columns are slightly narrower than news columns, to allow for the borders.)

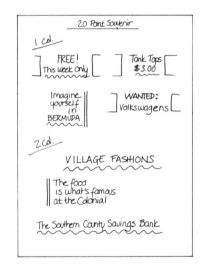

When specifying type for ad makeup, a designer will sometimes make up an ad dummy (left) to help visualize what type sizes and styles to use. Above, the spec sheet that will be given to the typographer.

Then write down on these sheets all the ad copy you'll need set, under the correct category. Mark everything you write down as completely as possible—if you want the material centered, flush right, flush left, or set with extra leading, *say so*. If you have your own phototypesetting equipment, get to know which combinations of typefaces and sizes are easiest for the typesetter to combine. If you have a filmstrip with both Helios and Helios Bold on it, for example, take advantage of this fact by designing ads with the two fonts in combination, and specify the type on a single sheet for the typographer. This can save a great deal of pasteup work. This is the time for you (and your typographer) to learn the copy editor's symbols (see page 32) and to use them clearly.

Perhaps you're sending your ad specifications out (if you don't have photocomposition equipment). Perhaps you're setting the ad copy yourself. But even if the person who sets your type has a Ph.D. in English literature, always remember the cardinal rule of specifications: *Assume the typographer is a complete idiot. Mark it exactly the way you want it.* Circle anything you don't want set, such as little notes to the idiot at the keyboard.

Laying out the ads. Next, on blank layout sheets, measure out and draw in nonreproducible blue pencil the outlines of each ad that is to be laid out. Label each one in blue pencil with the advertiser's name. Don't skimp or expand on the standard ad widths you have set; it will give a ragged appearance to the finished page if you do. And don't deal in half-inch heights unless you charge by that standard; if you charge in full inches, expand or reduce the ad to be an even number of inches high. Otherwise you'll run into problems blocking several ads on the page.

When you get the typeset copy from the compositor, cut it and distribute it onto the proper ad blocks that you have drawn up. Then paste it carefully into position, along with any artwork that belongs in the ad.

Often an advertiser will give you a piece of art or a photograph that he or she wants included in an ad. Your ad representative should be trained to reject material that won't reproduce well (see pages 112–113)—photographs that have been clipped from other newspapers; printed material or art in light blue, violet, yellow, or light grey; color photographs that won't come out well in black and white (a red dress on a dark background, for example). If it's borderline, either call the advertiser and ask if you can substitute something else, or put in a blackout for the art, label it clearly for placement and percentage of reduction or enlargement, and include it with the material that the printer will shoot separately. (See discussion of enlargements and reductions on pages 97–98.)

To reverse an ad or a portion of an ad, put in a blackout where it should be in the paper, label it with the percentage of enlargement or reduction, if any, write "reverse" on the label, and include it separately for the printer. (If you have a photostat camera available, you can make reverses yourself.)

Once the ads are pasted up on the sheets, put on the borders (see page 93); cut out the ads, trimming the border tape neatly; and place them on the newspaper page layout sheets where you'll want them to go.

Preliminary ad placement. Obviously, a small-format page must have fewer ads than a standard-size page in order not to look crowded. You are trying for a clean, uncluttered appearance that will give primary visual importance to the news and editorial matter, while still making the ads readable and attractively placed. There are several ways you can achieve this end:

¶ Block the ads—that is, square them off—at the bottom of the page where possible. Where you can, it's also nice to balance ad blocks on facing pages.

¶ Avoid stacking larger ads. We try never to stack ads that are more than five inches high. When you are stacking ads, it's better to put the larger one beneath the smaller one.

¶ The smallest ads often look best if they are grouped together in a certain section of the paper. We put them on our classified ad pages, which have a very high readership; people get used to this placement and look for smaller ads there.

¶ Very large ads—half-page and over—will attract enough attention without being placed in "prime" positions. We tend to put them on left-hand pages.

¶ If you have an ad that requires a two-page spread, you will be forced to use the newspaper's centerfold; we prefer to keep this spot free for our main feature story.

¶ Keep certain pages free of ads—the editorial page, the front page, photo features, and the like.

¶ In general, avoid placing competitive ads together. Exceptions to this rule occur when advertisers would naturally want to be on a particular page: sporting equipment ads on the sports page, food and restaurant ads on the appropriate pages, movie ads on the review page, and so forth.

¶ Try to keep ads below the fold in the page, where possible, and always try to have an ad at the foot of every column, except on open pages.

Bigger ads create more flexibility in layout than do smaller ones; an edition with one or more full-page ads will look better than one with the same amount of advertising space divided up into a lot of small ads. Big ads free more pages for open-page layout. Smaller ads always cost more—in layout, in billing, in placement, and often even in collection.

The ideal inside page will have one rectangle of advertising and another rectangle of editorial matter. This arrangement will give the most flexibility for the use of pictures and for imaginative layout schemes.

Don'ts. Certain ad placements always look bad.

¶ Don't fill a column by piling up small ads. Leave at least 2½ inches and preferably 4 inches at the top of every page, unless you have a full-page ad or one of less than full-page width that reaches to the top of the page. If an ad reaches almost to the top, don't run one inch of copy over it. Float the ad between the top and the bottom of the type page, and charge for the full column. (And tell your ad representative to avoid selling ads of that height.)

 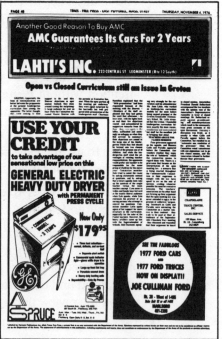

At left, ads fill the outside column of a four-column page, which distracts attention from editorial matter and gives the primary focus to advertising. At right, the cardinal sin of page makeup—a big, black, full-width ad is placed across the top of a page, directly over editorial matter.

¶ Don't create a "well" for editorial matter by stacking ads in a double pyramid.

¶ Don't build a column of ads on the outside of the page, with editorial copy on the inside columns. This is called "magazine placement," and gives priority to ads over reading matter.

¶ Don't place an ad, or part of an ad, directly above editorial matter on the same page. In particular, don't float ads as islands in the middle of reading matter, and don't spread an ad across the top of the page with reading matter underneath.

ARRANGING THE MATERIAL ON THE PAGES

Once the ads are laid out and pasted up, and you have positioned them on blank layout sheets approximately in the places you will want them, it is time to start positioning editorial copy—that is, news, pictures, features, and the like. Because each small newspaper has its own distinctive format—page size, number of columns, constant elements—it is impossible in a book of this sort to give specific instructions for this stage of layout. In addition, this stage involves a good deal of visual judgment, which can be an instinctive rather than a rulebook procedure.

One can, however, make rules of thumb about what kinds of copy will occupy the different spaces in each issue of the newspaper. We choose, for example, to place our main feature story on the right side of the center-fold—or across the entire centerfold if its length warrants. We cluster most of the important or "hard" news towards the front of the paper, breaking it up with pictures and news features. Our editorial page is always page 2, often overflowing onto page 3 with letters and opinion columns. (Many newspapers put their editorials on the back page, or the next-to-last pages.) Our "softer" features, such as reviews, gardening, birdwatching, and food columns, and social items are usually placed towards the back of the paper. Classified ads and sports news bring up the rear.

As well as such broad placement guidelines, there are certain other principles that can guide a layout editor. All of these, not surprisingly, revolve around the goal of *making it easy for the reader.* The same impulse that leads us to select for our columns the line length that will be easiest to read makes us strive to organize our pages so that the reader can move easily through a story, can scan a page quickly to determine what interests him or her, can be entertained rather than distracted by editorial art and pictures. Some of these basic principles are listed here.

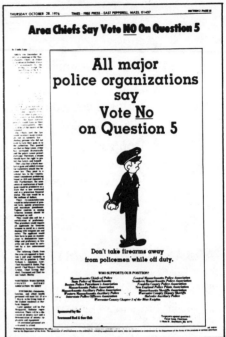

Confusing layout of the page at left has caused the story to begin in the second column and continue in the first and finally the third. At right, not only does the article's headline extend beyond the one-column copy it covers, but the story is placed directly next to a paid advertisement on the same subject, conveying the distinct impression that the editorial space has been "bought" along with the ad.

Blocked ads. Arranging ads so that they form rectangular or square blocks on the page, rather than letting them straggle up and down columns, will add to the visual simplicity of the small-format page. This is desirable even if your ad columns are of the same width as your copy columns; it is essential if these two widths are different.

The ad pyramid. The ad pyramid should be built so that what journalism schools call the *primary optical area*—the outer top corners of the page that attract the reader's eyes first and longest—are left free for editorial copy or art. Especially in a small-format newspaper, you can't afford to waste this space on ads—unless, of course, a full-page ad leaves you no choice.

The "reading diagonal." Experts in newspaper design refer to the way in which the reader's eye moves through the page as the "reading diagonal." Starting at the top left corner of a two-page spread, they say, the eye moves to the lower right corner; in order to attract the eye to the copy not directly in that line, the layout editor must position "magnets" in the form of headlines or other display elements.

Never run a headline past the text matter that it accompanies. At left, heading stretches ludicrously on, extending over an ad on the same page. The page at right illustrates two reasons not to run advertising adjacent to editorial art. Not only is the eye confused by the two graphic stimuli, but the ad matter implies to the subconscious that the wedding couple portrays the "bargain of the month."

Separation of ads from editorial art. Because ads and editorial art compete with each other for the reader's attention, they should always be separated by type areas. A picture placed directly above an ad will register in the reader's unconscious as advertising art and will be skipped over. This is not to say that your readers don't read the ads; they generally do pay close attention to advertising material. But they like to know just what is ad matter and what is not; it is your responsibility to make the distinction clear by keeping the ads and the editorial art away from each other.

Separation of stories. Make it easy for your reader to decide what to read by arranging the stories on the page in a varied but simple way. Avoid "tombstoning"—running two headlines, especially single-column heads, side by side; the stories can be separated by a one-column picture or a boxed bit of copy and the problem will be solved. If you are forced to run two headlines side by side, use contrasting type styles—roman and italic, for example.

Length of type blocks. Take care to make your columns of copy a readable length, neither too short nor too long. It looks silly and awkward to have a headline across several columns with only a few lines of type in each column underneath; make a rule that no fewer than eight lines of type should go under a head. It also makes it hard on your reader to have to plow through long columns of unbroken copy. Break the type into shorter column lengths, or jump the story to another page if necessary. If you must run long columns of type, break the story with subheads, pictures, or boxed inserts—or consider whether the article could best be divided into two separate stories, as with a long committee-meeting report.

Jumps. Though jumping a story—continuing it on another page—is a useful layout technique, it is, again, distracting to the reader. Avoid too many jumped articles in one issue; and never jump more than once within one article. If you go back and start over at the beginning of the layout problem, you can usually find another way to arrange the copy so that a double jump is unnecessary. When you do jump a story, continue it on a page that is easy for the reader to turn to—the next page is best, or the back page. You should have a jump line on both pages ("continued on page 5," "continued from page 3") set in a way that differentiates it from the text—in italic, in bold, or in parentheses, for example.

Pictures above type. Pictures should always be placed above the type in the story they accompany. A headline can go over the whole story and picture; but if you do this, be sure that the story begins directly under the first words of the headline.

Columns of type within a story. The type within a story should follow naturally, column after column; one should never have to skip from column one to column three, even if an accompanying picture fills column two. Place pictures so that they complement the text, not interfere with it.

Copy adjacent to advertisements. Be conscious of possible embarrassing juxtapositions. We try to avoid putting liquor-store ads next to court news of drunk drivers, just as we avoid putting ads for two competing banks side by side. We've been asked to run gravestone manufacturers' ads next to the obituaries, but we just feel that it's in bad taste. We almost always decline to promise ad placements. At the same time, we will try to put food-related ads on the recipe page, and the like. Use your judgment.

Naked columns. Naked columns are those without a headline or a picture at the top. They look awkward on the page and should be avoided.

Boxed copy. Boxing small stories provides a visual element that is very pleasant as an alternative to pictures or editorial art. We use one- or two-point rules to do this, either on all four sides, as with our calendars of upcoming events, or simply top and bottom, in which case we can use a

Layout of a page with no ads is illustrated by the front page at left, where the eye moves from the upper left corner through the stories and ends at the picture in the lower right. Lower left corner is "anchored" by index; boxed copy would serve the same purpose. In the page at right, the lack of editorial art is made up for by an attractive and varied use of display type for headlines and pullouts as well as thin and heavy rules.

more decorative rule. Another attractive device is to outline photographs with a hairline rule to set them off from adjacent matter.

Using these visual principles, layout of any page can proceed fairly logically. Here is how to place copy on a page with no ads, like the front page:

► First, fill the top left corner—the "primary optical area"—with an attention-getter. A picture is best, but you don't always want your layout to be the same, so just choose something that deserves the prominent position.

► Next, place the main story, if it didn't go in the top left corner. Traditionally, this goes in the top right corner.

► Then arrange your secondary stories on the page to lead down to the lower right corner, following the "reading diagonal" described earlier.

► Finally, anchor your lower left corner with a strong item: the beginning of a softer feature, a secondary picture, or the like.

When you're doing a page with ads, follow the same basic procedures. If you don't have a picture to be the attention-getter on a page, you'll have a tougher job of maintaining reader interest by providing "magnets" to lead the eye down the page; but imaginative headlines or "pullouts" (arresting excerpts set in display type), boxed copy, or logos that accompany regular columns can do the same thing.

Strive for a feeling of balance to the page. If all the elements were actually weighted in proportion to their bigness and boldness, would the finished page, suspended, tilt radically to one side or another?

HEADLINES

After the copy is all positioned on the pages and has been pasted up carefully (see pages 95–99) with space left for appropriate heads, we write headlines. This is easier because we know exactly how much space we have for each headline; if a story is a bit squeezed we can write a head of only one line; a story stretching over several columns can get a long head, and so forth. Also, it makes it much easier to set headlines in type styles that complement each other and present a varied but unified look on the page. If you have had to "tombstone" two stories, you can at least give them contrasting heads.

As with ads, we are conservative when it comes to type styles for headlines; we limit ourselves to the use of four or five fonts, and reserve the fancier of these for features rather than for news stories. Whatever your typographic preference for the face of your paper—bold or light, breezy or sober—your choice should be limited. Used well, this technique can pull the overall appearance of the newspaper together, give it a unified feeling, and do much towards establishing an image that will remain in people's minds. Papers that indiscriminately scatter vastly different headline styles throughout their pages come off looking like someone went through the trash to find the pieces that made them up.

Some examples of headline type styles you could choose:

¶ sans-serif bold, roman and italic, with a condensed and a light of the same sans-serif type for variation;

¶ serif bold alternating with sans-serif bold and bold italic;

¶ serif light and bold, roman and italic, with a sans-serif light and bold for special features.

Any regular column, of course, could have its own special display type that serves as its logo, identifying it as a constant feature.

The newspaper at left chooses a large, bold headline style, and breaks up the type page by the use of subheads and excerpts from the article set in a smaller display type. This is a useful alternative when pictures are lacking. At right, a good example of how to use one traditional type style imaginatively in headlines to keep a varied but unified appearance.

Length of headlines. The headline over a one-column story shouldn't exceed three lines; a two-column story shouldn't get more than a two-decker head. A story spreading across three or more columns can easily take a larger-than-usual type size in its headline, but should usually have just a one-line head.

Justified or copyfit headlines. There are ways to "copy-fit" your headlines so that the words exactly fill up all the space available; they can teach you how to do this in journalism schools. At the Harvard Post we prefer simply to let common sense prevail, perhaps because at three in the morning, when we're usually writing our headlines, we just can't face a character count. Instead, we just write the heads in a way that we think will fit; the typographer yells at us if we're wrong, and we work on it some more. Because we stick to a small number of headline fonts, we've grown to be able to estimate pretty well. It is best to have the headline fill up as much of the available space as possible; this can usually be done by choosing your words carefully. If the head has more than one line, balance the lines so that they are approximately equal; never leave a single word all alone on a line.

We center our one-column headlines on the column; this is an old-fashioned look, not favored by those who copy-fit their headlines, but we like it. With two-column heads, sometimes we center the lines on two columns, and other times we make the first line flush left and the second line flush right. Headlines that run across three or more columns we position flush left.

Caps or lower-case? Never set an entire headline all in capitals, though it can be a useful device to set a short teaser line in caps as a preface to a longer headline (*THE BIRD CENSUS: Titmice Outnumber Cardinals Again*). Modern newspapers often set their headlines completely in lower-case letters, except for the first word of the head and any words that are normally capitalized. We prefer, again, the more old-fashioned style, capitalizing everything but articles, conjunctions, and prepositions of fewer than five letters.

Pullout quotes. Another eye-catching use of headline type is to break up a long article with short passages pulled from the piece. This can serve many functions: it draws the reader into the story with attention-getting tidbits; it relieves the monotony of body type and moves the eye along, especially if you are short on pictures; it allows you to emphasize key points without necessarily putting them in the main headline; and it helps when you are laying out an article that's a bit too short for the space you have planned. Don't feel that you must stick exactly to the wording as it appears in the text of the article; a little editing for length is permissible here as long as the pull-out is substantially correct and you have not put words into someone's mouth.

Some warnings. Never put a headline over material to which it doesn't refer—over an ad, over another article's head, over an unrelated picture. The headline over the continued portion of a jumped story should either repeat the headline from the first part of the article or consist of a key word or phrase (*School Committee Meeting* or *Stolen Car*) that enables the reader to identify the continuation easily.

Take a good look at your headlines to make sure they say what you want them to say. An unfortunate line break can result in a head that is embarrassingly easy to misread (*Town Virgin / Lands on Agenda*); too-zealous "headlinese" can lead to dropping so many words that the resulting head is ridiculous (*Denies Club Fights Teens' Plans*). And sometimes the pressure of a deadline will simply blind you to the ludicrous double meaning of the headline you've just written: *Sewer Input Sought* or *Robber Holds Up Albert's Hosiery* or *Milk Drinkers Turn to Powder*. Don't let it happen to you.

7 Pasteup

PASTING UP YOUR CAMERA–READY COPY must be a meticulous process; and although we have done it with gloves on in a Volkswagen bus in the middle of a snowstorm with a hungry three-year-old bouncing in the back, it is far better to arrange a clean, well-lighted, and efficiently organized area in which to work. Remember: every spot of peanut butter and every inky fingerprint will photograph and reproduce, to embarrass you in the finished product. And though a careful printer will watch for such carelessness and opaque it out on the negative, it is your responsibility to present the printer with immaculate copy. (We have seen a newspaper with the outline of a paper clip printed along its edge; and another where a formal wedding portrait was defaced by a misplaced scrap of ad copy that read VEGETABLES in large type right below the faces of the smiling couple.)

MATERIALS

Layout sheets. For accurate pasteup, good ruled layout sheets are the most important tools. You should have drawn up, and printed by your printer in nonreproducible ink, large sheets of heavy white paper with your columns marked off vertically in exact measure. These sheets should also be ruled horizontally in intervals of no more than one-half inch, to assist you in

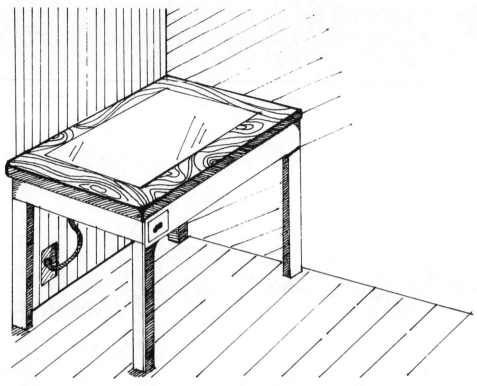

A light table.

aligning your copy. Many newspapers use layout sheets gridded into one-pica squares, or having horizontal rules at intervals equal to the depth of a line of the paper's standard type—every nine or ten points, for example. It is also helpful to have special layout sheets drawn up for pages that regularly have their own individual design, such as the editorial or classified ad pages.

Layout tables. It is essential to have some large area on which you can spread out all the pages of your newspaper, in sequence, as you are laying it out and pasting it up. For years the Harvard Post got along with the kitchen counter and the living-room floor; but ever since we had our layout tables built we've been a lot more agreeable on deadline day. Make sure your layout tables are long enough to accommodate layout sheets for the largest number of pages you're likely to put out in one issue. The tables should be slightly slanted, but not so much that the pages fall off; a little lip attached to the bottom edge keeps pencils and knives from rolling off. Other handy features of a good layout table are large shelves underneath to hold extra layout sheets and the like, and a small shelf overhead to hold rubber cement and other supplies.

Light table. Also indispensable for good pasteup work is the light table; when you lay the lined layout sheets onto it you can paste up your copy neatly because the faint blue lines will show right through. Light tables are expensive to buy (though you can occasionally find a good used one for very little), but easy and cheap to make. To build a small, portable light table you'll need a piece of ¼-inch-thick frosted glass or white acrylic about 20 inches by 30 inches—a surface big enough upon which to lay out a two-page spread. Then you simply build a box of wood about 6 or 8 inches deep, using perhaps ¾-inch-thick boards or plywood and leaving the top of the box open. Then nail or glue another thin strip of wood around the inside of the box; its distance below the box's top edge should be just the thickness of your glass or acrylic. The material you use for your working surface can thus rest on this ledge and at the same time be flush with the top edge of the box, making it possible to use a T-square without interference. Even nicer is to build the table so that the working surface tilts slightly towards you—just enough to make working over it more comfortable, but not so much that the materials with which you're working slide off.

Before dropping the glass or acrylic into place, though, you must install a light fixture in the bottom of the box; a fluorescent fixture (or two) is preferred because it provides a more diffuse light beneath your working surface. It's best to install a light switch in the side of the box. And it's essential to drill some holes in the sides of the box for ventilation; otherwise the light table could become dangerously hot. (A good, detailed plan for a small light table like the one described here can be found in *Building Craft Equipment* by A. J. and Carol W. Abrams, published by Praeger in 1976.)

Rubber cement. Some people prefer rubber cement to wax in the pasting up of copy, mainly because there is less chance that the copy will detach itself from the layout sheets between you and the printer. But rubber cement is messier, and it can be difficult to move copy that has already been cemented down if you change your mind about positioning. If you use rubber cement, observe the following rules:

¶ Use a light, even coat of rubber cement on the back of each piece of copy. Less glue will make copy easier to lift up if you have to. Don't use globs of heavy glue once your bottle has thickened; either thin the rubber cement or use a fresh bottle.

¶ Make meticulous use of a *rubber cement pickup eraser.* When rubber cement dries on your layout sheets it often picks up dirt from your fingers, and all this dirt will photograph. A pickup eraser is a small stiff rubbery square that will pick up all the extra rubber cement from the paper. Ours is always disappearing, and we have found that in emergencies a ball made of old thick rubber cement will make a fair substitute.

There is a spray-on rubber cement available in cans, and many pasteup people prefer to use it. The fumes it creates annoy us, though; and we always have the uneasy feeling that we may be coating our lungs as well as our copy with particles of glue.

Wax. If you decide to use hot wax instead of rubber cement, you will need to buy an electric waxer. The wider table-top waxers, through which the copy runs on rollers, cost at least three hundred dollars, and it's hard to find used ones for sale. Ours is the Artwaxer, which we bought through the Dick Blick graphic supply catalogue. A small hand waxer can be bought for about thirty dollars; it's adequate, but can be a little messy, and the strip of wax you get is only 1 ½ inches wide.

Wax is cleaner than rubber cement, and it is easier to move copy around when you see a better solution to a layout puzzle. If you have slanted layout tables, waxed copy has the additional advantage of staying where you put it in the tentative layout stage. If you use wax, always *burnish* your pages when you have made the final pasteup. Simply put a piece of tracing paper or other thin sheet over the entire page, and rub evenly and hard over the pasted up areas with a burnishing tool or a broad, flat surface that will not tear your copy.

T-square. This indispensable tool is used in lining up copy so that it is straight on the page. It must be used with a straight edge—attached to your light table or layout board—to be accurate. With the head of the T-square held snugly against the left edge of your surface, the ruler section of the T-square should line up directly with your copy. It's a good idea always to make a final check of pasted up copy with the T-square, even if you are using a light table and gridded paper. Nothing is more annoying to a reader's eye than crooked copy.

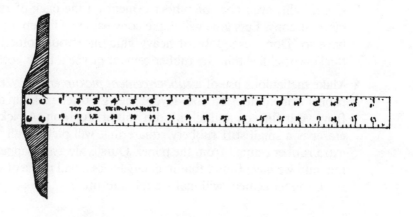

The T-square.

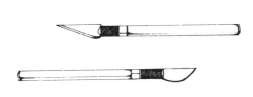

Proportional scale.   *Artist's razor knife.*

Good metal rulers. You'll need good stainless steel rulers, 18 inches long, with markings for inches, picas (and half-picas), and agate lines. Plastic rulers tend to warp, although there is one excellent 12-inch translucent model with one-point markings, very useful for specifying type.

Reducing wheel or proportional scale. A reducing/enlarging wheel is a proportional slide rule consisting of two circular laminated disks about six inches in diameter. It's used to calculate the percentage at which you want the printer to shoot your photographs. (See pages 97–98.)

Artist's razor knife. Have several of these precision cutting tools around, with a supply of fresh blades. They're most often called X-acto knives, after the main company that makes them, and they're indispensable for trimming, cutting between lines, moving around small bits of copy, and a thousand other things (including slitting wrists as deadlines pass).

Nonreproducible blue pencils and pens. Lay in a supply of nonreproducible blue pencils for marking up your layout sheets to your heart's content. Get a felt-tip nonreproducible blue pen, and you can mark your typographical errors right on the copy without fear of messing up a good line by accident.

Red or black grease pencils. You'll need grease pencils (china markers) in colors that reproduce, to make crop-marks on photographs.

Paper cutter. An 18-inch table-top paper cutter is big enough; smaller than that, they tend to be inaccurate. Get the best one you can afford.

Scissors. Have at least three good pairs of sharp scissors. They get lost easily. It's nice if at least one pair has extra-long blades for cutting long strips of copy.

Border tapes. One of the easiest ways to make clean, straight rules in your paper—for ad borders, for cutoff rules, for boxed copy—is to use one of a variety of commercial border tapes. These are available on rolls; you lay them down where you want them and they stick. Stretch the tape over the area to be covered, touch it down at one or two points, then quickly smooth it down with your finger. Trim the edges neatly with a razor knife, and even if you can't draw a straight line your readers will never know it.

Transfer lettering. When you need display type that is larger than or of a different style from that provided by your regular typesetter, transfer lettering is a convenient way to get it. It comes on large master sheets and is rubbed directly onto a white sheet of paper and burnished to hold its place. Some of the major manufacturers of transfer lettering are Letraset, Mecanorma, and Chartpak; but keep your eyes open for new kinds. The selection of available typefaces and sizes is enormous.

Transfer lettering tends to crack and peel, especially if you're unlucky and get an old sheet; we generally cover the completed lettering with a matte-finish tape such as Scotch Magic Tape. Always do transfer lettering on a lined layout sheet so that you have an accurate guideline for the baselines of the letters. Letterspacing guides are often provided on the sheets; but sometimes they're inaccurate, so trust your own eyes—and watch the baseline.

Where to get supplies. We get almost all the supplies we need from Charrette Corporation, an excellent art and graphics supply store in the Boston area. They do a large mail-order business, and you can get their catalogue by writing to Charrette, 31 Olympia Avenue, Woburn, Massachusetts 01801. Another excellent graphic supply house is Dick Blick, Box 1267, Galesburg, Illinois 61401.

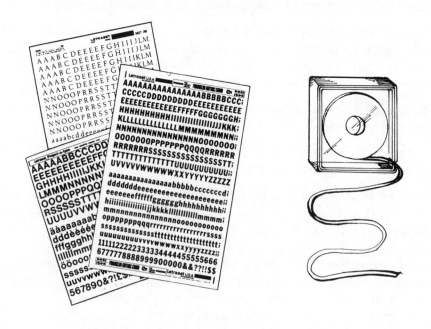

Transfer lettering.   *Package of border tape.*

PROCEDURES

Proofread all your copy carefully; we mark the errors directly on the copy in nonreproducible blue ink. When all the copy has been read for errors, the typographer can set corrections all at once. Always have at least two lines of copy set for a correction, and preferably three; this makes it much easier to paste in. Trim the correction carefully so that it will not obscure the descenders and ascenders of the letters on the lines above and below it; and then position it directly over the lines containing the error. (This is easier than cutting out the incorrect lines, and makes it easier to line up the copy. It should be done on a light table for greatest accuracy.) Never try to strip in just one letter, one word, or even one line. It invariably turns out crooked. Make sure the edges of the correction are pasted down flat to avoid shadows.

Trim your lengths of copy from the typesetter carefully, especially where a break occurs within an article. Nothing looks so amateurish as an uneven gap where an article has been patched together. When you do have to paste up two sections of an article that are on separate lengths of copy, take special care that the spacing between the lines is the same as if it had all been set in one length. This can be done by measuring the distance in points from the base of one line to the base of the next. If your copy is set, for example, in 9-point type on 10 points of space, you should be able to measure a 10-point space between the base of one line and the base of the next. A good metal or translucent plastic pica ruler will have measurements for several different point sizes on it as well as for picas. (It looks even worse to have lines of copy squeezed too close together than it does to have a bit of extra space. Don't err on this side.)

If you have a light table and are working with ruled layout paper with your column size marked on it, the pasteup job should be simple. Just align the columns according to the rules, keeping the copy straight both horizontally and vertically.

Spacing. Now is the time to pay strict attention to the spacing of various elements of your newspaper page. The amount of white space that should be left around headlines varies according to the weight of your headline style, and other spacing decisions will be determined in part by the overall typographic design of your newspaper. But certain conventions should be observed:

¶ More space should be left above a headline than between the headline and the story. A minimum of six points of space must be left between headline and story.

¶ Spacing between the lines of a headline should always be uniform.

Town Slowly Digs Out From the Century's Worst Blizzard

by Valentine Rathbone

Harvard, along with the rest of eastern Massachusetts, was hit by a blizzard of historic proportions on Monday and Tuesday this week. The storm brought travel and commerce to a standstill for several days; on Thursday many people were still digging out.

A Classic Nor'easter

The snow began lightly late Monday morning, and Boston weather forecasters began to predict a classic nor'easter of up to three days' duration. By Monday evening the snow was falling at the rate of about one inch per hour, and there were gale force winds as well, making travel

Headline: 18 on 20

Under head: 1 pica

Under byline: 5 points

Body copy: 9 on 9.5

Above subhead: 5 points

Below subhead: 3 points

¶ A half-line space (that is, half the amount of vertical space allowed for each line of copy) should be left between byline and story when it is set in single-column width. A whole line space should be left when the type is set in a wide measure.

¶ At least a pica of space should be left above a picture; and at least six points of space between a picture and its caption. If you come closer, the tape your printer uses to strip in the negative will blur the caption or credit line. Even if you are prescreening your own pictures, you need six points visual space between the picture and the caption.

¶ Leave at least a pica of space above and below boxed material, and at least six points of space between the sides of a box and the material within. Make sure that the sides of a box don't come too close to the copy in adjacent columns of type.

¶ Headlines should not be allowed to fill up a wider space than the story underneath.

¶ Subheads within a story should have about a half-line space above and a three-point space below them. Don't balance them equally between copy above and below.

¶ If you find yourself with an inch to spare at the end of a story, you have several options. You can "paragraph space" your story as big newspapers do, adding a uniform amount of space

—no more than two points, please!—between paragraphs to space it out. We don't like the way this looks, though, and prefer to add a little more space between stories, or to set a short news item or filler ("Post Classifieds: 2 Weeks for a Dollar; Call 456-8122") separated by a rule from the copy above.

Cutoff rules. Sometimes it will be necessary to use a cutoff rule—a horizontal divider of plain one-point border tape—to make clear a division. These will occur, for example, when the headline under a picture is unrelated to the art, or when portions of two separate stories are included in a single column of type without a headline to divide them.

Blackouts. You will have to paste onto your camera-ready layout sheet a black, red, or orange piece of paper exactly the desired size of each photograph or piece of copy that the printer has to shoot separately and strip in. (This includes not only photographs but also artwork that must be reduced or enlarged, reversed copy, or even type that you're having the printer enlarge or reduce.) Put the blackout exactly where you want the photograph or copy stripped in. The best material for blackouts is Rubylith acetate; but red, orange, or black paper with a glossy finish will do fine. Label each blackout with the number of the page it's on and with a letter to distinguish it from other blackouts on the same page, and put the same number-letter label on the picture or copy to be shot separately.

Preparing photographs for the printer. First, decide what area of the photograph you want to reproduce. Crop-marks should be indicated with red or black grease pencil on the white border of the print. (If there's no border, stick the picture lightly with a few dabs of rubber cement to a larger white sheet and make the crop-marks on the white paper.)

Next, calculate the percentage of enlargement or reduction you need to fit the picture into the space you have available. This is done with a circular proportional scale that works like a slide rule. Follow these steps:

1. Write down the dimensions of the part of the photo that you want to reproduce. (If you're starting with a 5- by 7-inch print and you aren't cutting out any part of the picture, write down 5 inches by 7 inches.) Width is always written first.

2. Then write down the *width,* in inches, of the area where you want to place the photograph in the paper. (If you have a two-column space available, write down the width of two of your columns.) You now have something like this:

5 inches by 7 inches

4½ inches by ?

3. Now use the proportional scale to get the missing dimension. Match up the original width on the "original size" disk of the scale with the desired width on the outer disk. Then check where the original height is on the inner disk; it should match up with a new dimension on the outer disk, which will be the desired height. In a window near the center of the disk, an arrow will point to the percentage of reduction or enlargement you have calculated. (In the example above, the reduction is 90 percent, and the reproduction height is about 6¼ inches.)

4. Making sure that you write somewhere between the cropmarks so that the printer will see it clearly, mark the white border of the photograph (or a tag attached to the photo) with the percentage of enlargement or reduction. Then label both the blackout and the photograph with a page number and an identifying letter (see above).

If you're including several very similar photographs on a page—mug shots of political candidates, for example, or houses in real estate ads—mark additional instructions for the printer ("top left," or the like). And if a photo or piece of art could easily be turned the wrong way by the printer, label the top of the picture for his information.

Photo marked for cropping. Picture itself should not be cut; the printer will trim the negative according to the crop-marks.

Final check. Check over your final pasteup carefully. You are looking for:

¶ smudged areas or dirty rubber cement (use white liquid opaquing fluid to cover smudges if they don't erase);

¶ faded or yellowing type areas; your copy should be of uniform darkness to reproduce best when the printer photographs it;

¶ uneven spacing between lines of headlines;

¶ misplaced copy; everywhere there is a break within an article, check to make sure the right copy follows;

¶ corrections to strip in; make sure, again, that the correction does not obscure other copy and that it has been put in the right place;

¶ correct labeling of blackouts to correspond with material to be stripped in. Every blackout in the final pasteup must have a corresponding piece of art or photograph to go with it. Make sure these are accurately labeled by page number and letter so that the printer can match photo and blackout easily;

¶ correct dates and page numbers on each page;

¶ missing captions, credit lines, bylines, and anything else that was supposed to be pasted in separately and might have been overlooked;

¶ correct number of pages (it's all too easy to rush off to the printer minus page one, which is sitting at the typographer's table where it was taken for a correction).

Finally, use the T-square or the light table to check carefully all alignment throughout the paper. Remember: straight copy, with uniformly sized gutters between the columns and neatly aligned headlines, is perhaps the most important element in a fine-looking newspaper. Purists who decry the advent of cold type and offset-printed newspapers most often point to sloppy pasteup as one of the chief sins of the new methods. Your meticulous work can combat their prejudices more than any amount of verbal battle.

8 Advertising

ADVERTISING IS OF CRUCIAL IMPORTANCE to any newspaper (unless it is an in-house corporate paper, is supported by a nonprofit organization, or is otherwise subsidized). Newspapers that circulate by means of paid subscriptions and newsstand sales generally derive 70 to 80 percent of their income from advertising. Those that are distributed free, of course, are supported totally by advertising. Advertisements also take up a goodly percentage of the space in most newspapers, which means that the appearance of a publication's ads will in large part determine its graphic style. Finally, selling advertising is one of the most challenging jobs in the production of a small newspaper; it involves intelligence and psychological awareness equal to that of any good reporter. If you recognize the importance of the advertising content of your newspaper—both in quantity and quality—you will be able to balance it with an equally high caliber of editorial content.

Postal regulations limit the amount of advertising in second-class matter to 75 percent, but we keep our ad percentage much lower than that, by choice. We believe that more than 50 percent advertising in a small-format newspaper with a limited number of pages looks trashy and lowers the quality of the newspaper by limiting its editorial content. "Experts" may tell you that no newspaper averaging less than 65 percent advertising can survive, but the Harvard Post has been doing quite well enough with about 45 percent. When we go over our rough 50 percent advertising limit in an issue, we generally prefer to add four more pages rather than to crowd the paper with ads.

Advertising is measured in *column inches*—a given ad will be so many columns wide by so many inches high. (Sometimes ad agencies or national advertisers will refer to an ad's height in *agate lines;* there are 14 agate lines to an inch.) An ad that measures, for example, two columns wide and four inches high is said to take up eight column inches. When you multiply the number of column inches by the rate you've decided to charge per column inch, you get the price of the ad.

Setting your rates. Setting your advertising rates will depend on many factors—how much it costs you to produce each issue, what the rates of your competitors are, and the like. We find that it's best to set a standard rate for all ads and stick to it, giving discounts only when an advertiser has run more than a certain amount of advertising in one month. (For example, our 1983 ad rate is $4.25 per column inch. If an advertiser's bill for ads taken in one calendar month exceeds $160, we give a 10 percent discount; if the ad is prepaid an automatic 5 percent discount is given. In addition, we offer a special "multiple prepayment" discount: 10 percent if the advertiser pays for three or more ads of any size in advance; 15 percent if six or more ads are paid for in advance. This gives even smaller advertisers a chance to qualify for a larger discount.

Many newspapers, however, have much more complicated rate schedules. They establish different rates for different kinds of advertising, and often give discounts based on frequency as well as volume. Whatever you do, make up a good, clear *rate card* or *rate sheet* explaining your charges and detailing all other advertising policies, to leave with merchants who may be interested in advertising. We raise our rates yearly on the same date; we notify our customers by printing up a new rate card (on a different color stock) and mailing it to everyone who has advertised in the past year.

Most newspapers offer substantial discounts on advertising rates if a contract is signed for a certain amount of advertising per year. (Such contracts, incidentally, are by custom cancellable at any time by the advertiser, although the newspaper is in such cases entitled to collect the difference between the discount rate and the rate that would normally have applied.) We have found that there is little benefit to signing an individual contract for each ad placed in the newspaper. It's time-consuming and complicated, and doesn't do much in any case to persuade a recalcitrant merchant to pay his overdue bill. Be scrupulous about making clear verbal contracts with your advertisers, keep good records, and you will find you have little need for short-term contracts.

Mechanical Requirements

PAGE SIZE

Our type page measures 10 inches wide by 15 inches long. There are four advertising columns on each page.

COLUMN SIZE

Each ad column measures 13½ picas in width. One-column ads are 2¼ inches wide; Two-column ads are 4¾ inches wide; Three-column ads are 7¼ inches wide; Four-column ads are 10 inches wide.

PHOTOS AND LINE DRAWINGS

Please provide clear black-and-white photos or artwork where possible. There is no extra charge for special layout work or for reproduction of halftones. We can provide photostatic copies of your finished ad if needed; there is a $5 added charge, per photostat, for this service.

PLACEMENT

Placement of ads is at the discretion of the layout editor; however, special requests will be accommodated wherever possible. No ads are ever placed on pages one or two.

Every advertiser will be mailed a complete copy of each issue containing his advertisement. Please notify us of errors or changes as soon as possible.

If you're looking for the best customers, you should advertise in the best newspaper.

Rates for Display Advertising

Effective October 1982

THE HARVARD POST
General Store Building
The Common
Harvard, Mass. 01451

The town of Harvard, located in northeastern Worcester County, near the intersection of Routes 2 and 495, has been long renowned for its apple orchards, its lovely landscape, and its fascinating history. Its hills, lakes, classic New England common, and unspoiled vistas make Harvard one of the most attractive small towns in Massachusetts. Over the years, its beauty and tranquility have attracted poets, philosophers, and visionaries, including the Shakers, Bronson Alcott and his transcendentalist friends, Fiske Warren, and others.

Today, Harvard continues to attract people with a taste for beauty, and its 4,600 citizens are, by and large, well educated and well-to-do. They enjoy the highest per-capita income in the county, and one of the highest in the state. They have demonstrated their concern for the town's future by preserving its historic areas and supporting a variety of environmental and conservation programs.

Harvard's residents also enjoy one of New England's most distinguished small newspapers—the Harvard Post. Now in its tenth year, the Post has become a town institution, read avidly by virtually every resident and by admirers in nearby communities and across the country.

THE HARVARD POST brings your advertising message to 6,000 discriminating readers every week. No other weekly or daily publication approaches the paid circulation of the Post in the Harvard market.

Basic display ad rate:
$4.25 per column inch

Typical Ad Sizes and Prices

Full Page		$255.00
Half Page		
Vertical	(2 columns x 15 inches)	127.50
Island	(3 columns x 10 inches)	127.50
Horizontal	(4 columns x 7 inches)	119.
Two-Fifths Page		
Vertical	(2 columns x 12 inches)	102.
Island	(3 columns x 8 inches)	102.
Horizontal	(4 columns x 6 inches)	102.
One-Third Page		
Vertical	(2 columns x 10 inches)	85.
Island	(3 columns x 7 inches)	89.25
Horizontal	(4 columns x 5 inches)	85.
One-Fourth Page		
Vertical	(2 columns x 7 inches)	59.50
Horizontal	(3 columns x 5 inches)	63.75
2 columns x 6 inches		51.
2 columns x 5 inches		42.50
2 columns x 4 inches		34.
2 columns x 3 inches		25.50
2 columns x 2 inches		17.
1 column x 3 inches		12.75
1 column x 2 inches		8.50

Remember: Because our columns are extra wide, you get more ad space for your dollar!

Pre-payment Discount

You may take an automatic 5 percent discount if you pay for your ad when you place it.

Special Multiple Pre-payment Discounts

The pre-payment discount becomes 10 percent if you pay for three or more ads in advance. They may be any size—even small ads qualify.

If you pay for six or more ads in advance, the pre-payment discount is 15 percent.

Volume Discount

Advertisers who choose to be billed for their ads will receive a 10 percent volume discount if the total bill for any one calendar month exceeds $160.

Advertising Agencies

Recognized advertising agencies will receive a 15 percent discount on ads that are delivered completely camera-ready. Pre-payment and volume discounts do not apply to agency accounts.

Volume and agency discounts will be extended only to accounts in good standing. Discounts may not be applied to payments received more than 30 days after billing, and overdue balances may be subject to a finance charge.

The Harvard Post's rate card is printed on 8½-by-11-inch index stock and folded twice. Each October, when we raise our ad rates, a new card is printed and mailed to every advertiser and potential advertiser.

Setting your ad column widths. The most common width for advertising columns is 10 to 11 picas, or 1¾ inches, which fits well with the most common 11-pica news column width in small-format papers. We choose to have our ad columns be the same width as our news columns, 2¼ inches or 13½ picas. If you choose a nonstandard width, you will have problems with ads prepared by agencies to a standard width, or clipped from other newspapers. We often find ourselves having to squeeze down or spread out ads prepared for 10- or 11-pica columns. On the other hand, we provide more space in our one-column width than most of our competitors do with their narrower columns; so we can justify a higher charge per column inch, and we think our ads look better as well.

Some newspapers with extra-wide news columns set up a system of different widths for advertising columns and news columns. They will squeeze perhaps six narrower columns of ads into the same space occupied by, say, three or four columns of news type. (The New York Times uses a system in which six columns of news take up the same space as nine columns of advertising.) This creates graphic problems: advertising must be "squared off" in such a way as to leave a rectangular area open at the top of the page for editorial copy. But there are financial advantages to this method, as ad revenues per newspaper page can be increased while column-inch rates seem lower.

An example of a four-column page with five columns of ads. The ads must be "blocked" to form a rectangle on the page.

An interesting example of this method can be seen by comparing the advertising rates of two small-format newspapers, the Maine Times and the New Hampshire Times. Both papers use a three-column design, both in editorial and advertising copy. The New Hampshire Times, however, says it has *six* columns of advertising—the catch is that it accepts ads only in two-, four-, and six-column widths. Though its ad rate, at $8.25 per column inch, *seems* cheaper than the Maine Times's rate ($14.42 per column inch), it's actually more expensive to place the same size ad in the New Hampshire paper.

The advertising representative. A good advertising representative is intelligent, friendly, personable, persistent, and not shy. He or she must be able to approach merchants week after week with good ideas, and must not feel personally affronted if the merchant turns down those ideas. The qualities present in a good salesperson are characteristic as well of a good advertising representative: filling the customer's real need for an imaginative, accurate representation of his goods and services. The publisher himself or herself is often the best ad rep to be had.

We pay our advertising representative a 16 percent commission on the ad revenues she or he brings in, plus a small sum each week to cover gasoline and telephone expenses. (See *Financial Matters,* pages 153–154, for a discussion of related bookkeeping.) This means that the ad rep earns more than anyone else on the staff. It's worth it; the paper depends on those ads.

Our representatives collect their commissions only when the ads have actually been paid for, which gives them an additional incentive to avoid selling to bad credit risks. Specific suggestions to help the ad representative on the job are included in this chapter on pages 110–111.

Puff pieces. Very often an advertiser will request that the newspaper print a "press release" having to do with "news" of his business—a new manager or employee, an open house, a contest, or the like. Unless such an item concerns a townsperson and can legitimately be included in your "People" section, it is best to maintain a strict policy against printing such material as news. If announcements of this kind are to be made, a paid advertisement is the place to make them.

As an alternative to the puff piece, many advertisers will offer to pay for having such an article set as news copy, with a headline, but inserted as an ad. You owe to your readers—and postal regulations require—a clear distinction between advertising and editorial content; yet the "news flash" is a legitimate advertising technique. When you accept such an ad, always follow these rules:

> ¶ Block off the "news story" ad with border rules, just as you would any other ad.

¶ Include the word "advertisement" at least once at the top of the ad, within the border, in a type at least as large as that used for the body copy of the ad, and easily legible to the reader.

¶ Set the "news story" and its headline in a *different type style* from that used for the real news in your paper.

The idea is to make it perfectly clear to your readers that this "news" is *not* an editorial offering, but paid advertising.

Position. Don't promise a particular position in the newspaper to an advertiser. The last-minute exigencies of layout often will make it impossible to keep such a promise, and you'll just create ill will among your advertisers by playing favorites. In any case, studies by advertising experts have shown that an ad's position doesn't affect its readership—even "buried" ads, if they are well designed, will attract attention. The advertiser who is worried about position should be persuaded to spend his energy creating good, clean, specific, and visually appealing ads; these are the ones, if any, that will receive the "best" placement in the newspaper.

Business directories. Many small papers have a regular page of small ads, classified for the reader's convenience and appearing in the same place each week. These ads are generaly about the size of a business card, or smaller, and are sold by yearly contract at a lower rate than usual.

Some newspapers also engage in the unfortunate practice of running a "feature story" on one of the businesses that advertise, as accompanying copy for the directory page. This serves no legitimate purpose, is usually a cheap ploy to attract advertisers, and in general does a disservice to readers. There is such a thing as legitimate business news coverage, the goal of which is to shed reportorial light on the progress, problems, and properties of business in your readership area; there is more on this subject in *Content,* page 13. But the editor of a good newspaper draws a strict line between advertising and news/editorial content, and the result is a loyal readership with a high rate of response to the paper's advertising.

Political advertisements. Political ads should always be paid for in advance. Making this a hard-and-fast rule keeps you from bearing the financial consequences when a candidate loses—and even winning candidates are frequently out of money. Many newspapers, in addition, charge a special rate, higher than all others, for political ads. Find out what the requirements are in your state for identifying the sponsors of the ad and for reporting campaign expenditures. In general, political ads must be labeled as such and must include the names of the people who are paying for them.

Classified ad page.

Business directory page, with "puff piece" about one of the advertisers.

Legal notices. Paid-circulation newspapers are eligible to carry legal advertising. This can come from any number of sources: local, county, state, and federal government agencies, including school boards, regulatory agencies, probate courts, and the like; banks, which advertise foreclosure sales and lost bankbooks; law firms; and various public and private institutions and societies. Many government agencies are required to advertise public hearings and invitations for bids on contracts. Find out what these requirements are in your area and actively solicit legal notices from the appropriate officials and boards. Especially if you are a new newspaper, just letting them know you exist will often result in their sending some advertising your way. Legal notices can command a higher rate than other advertising, and are often charged by the line rather than the inch.

Inserts. A common practice among small newspapers is the insertion of advertising pages as a separate section, or the "stuffing" of ad matter into the paper after it has been printed. Rates for this kind of advertising are generally much lower than for the same amount of ad copy within the newspaper proper, because the advertiser is responsible for the cost of making up and printing the insert. Most printers will agree to stuff the insert into the paper on a piecework basis, and your rates must of course reflect that cost. Newspapers generally charge by the piece for inserts.

We dislike this form of advertising; we feel that it takes advantage of our readers, foisting on them ad material that is not supported by editorial content. Also, because the special sections are usually designed and printed by the advertiser, the newspaper has little control over the graphic quality of the insert. All too often the appearance of an otherwise fine newspaper is cheapened by the inclusion of a garish advertising insert.

Moreover, the second-class mailing regulations of the United States Postal Service clearly prohibit such advertising inserts—although we were surprised to learn this, as almost every newspaper we know includes them. The regulations state in Section 425.54: "Parts or sections produced by someone other than the publisher may not be mailed at second-class rates if these parts or sections are prepared by or for advertisers or if they are provided to the publisher free or at a nominal charge." Apparently this regulation is never enforced, although you might want to try pointing it out to your local postmaster if advertising inserts in competing newspapers are hurting your business.

What should you say when an advertiser wants to run an insert? We suggest instead that our own ad and layout people design a full-page ad containing the same basic information.

If you decide that you want to try running an advertising insert and your paper is circulated through the mail, talk to your postmaster first about how to do it. There are several regulations that apply to separate sections of a newspaper; these may be found in Section 425 of the second-class mailing regulations. The name of your newspaper must be printed or stamped at the head of the insert to identify it as, technically, another section of your edition; and the number of sections in the edition must be printed on page one of the paper. (This can pose a problem if the insert is printed before it is placed with you; but you can have a rubber stamp made and stamp all the copies yourself.) The material in the insert is regarded as a "supplement" to the newspaper, and is required to be germane to the readership; in practice, we have not seen post offices turn down such material because it lacked editorial content. Every inch of the material in the supplement, finally, must be counted in the advertising percentage you report to the post office—even though you have collected much less money for it than for regular ad pages. Stuffers, clearly, are a can of worms that we feel is better left unopened.

Special sections or editions. Sometimes there will be an editorial reason to prepare a special section or edition of the newspaper—for the anniversary celebration of your town or group, for example; or for high school graduation; or to focus on a particular subject such as energy conservation, automobiles, or summer activities for children. The Harvard Post publishes a special edition at the end of every summer, for example, devoted to the literary and artistic contributions of staff and townspeople. Any such special section can be an opportunity for advertisers as well, and the advertising representative should bring it to their attention as early as possible. Even the most hardened naysayer will be reluctant to leave out his congratulatory ad when everyone else in town will be represented in the special graduation section; and everyone from insulation companies to drapery stores will be eager to see their ads in the energy conservation section. This can be an occasion to bring new advertisers into the fold, and to place their ads in a context that will do them the most good as well.

Advertising agencies. Many businesses, especially banks and chain stores, employ advertising agencies to design and place their advertising. These agencies select the media in which to advertise, and prepare camera-ready art and copy. They ask for a 15 percent discount off your regular advertising rate; then they collect from the merchant at the full ad rate, and pocket the 15 percent as their commission.

Dealing with agencies saves you layout time, but it can be a tricky business. Agencies think they know all there is to know about advertising, when in fact their taste is often no better than yours. They use only the broadest dollar-to-reader criteria for choosing the publications to advertise in, and so they often neglect the smaller newspaper with an exceptionally loyal readership. And they have a sometimes richly deserved reputation for procrastinating on payments. Make strict rules for dealing with ad agencies. They should receive a 15 percent discount only:

- ► if they supply complete camera-ready copy; you can charge them extra if they ask you to reduce or enlarge their copy, or to insert extra copy that you have to set into type;

- ► if they pay their bill within thirty days of the billing date.

Payment and credit. The advertising representative should keep in mind that there are always some businesspeople who will cheerfully take an ad in your newspaper with no intention of paying for it. Others will decide not to pay for their ad after it has run, claiming that the ad "didn't get any results." Learn who these accounts are and stay away from them; and be good to those advertisers who pay promptly, making sure they get their sample copies on time, visiting them to check how they liked the ad's appearance, and so forth.

Many newspapers require that new accounts pay for their ads in advance, although even this precaution is no defense against bouncing checks. If you have doubts about a new advertiser's reliability, ask for credit references and make a few telephone calls. Do not hesitate to demand advance payment—in cash or certified check, if necessary—if your investigations do not allay the doubts. Keep close tabs on advertisers' accounts, and don't let anyone run up an unreasonably high bill. These precautions should help you avoid most, but not all, bad debts. If you simply can't collect, you can take the scoundrel to court (even if you had no written contract with him, your verbal contract holds water); but though small-claims court may find you legally entitled to payment, it will do nothing to enforce its judgment and you may still be left righteously emptyhanded. More than once we have had to eat up unpaid advertising bills—literally—at delinquent restaurants, which as a group are notoriously poor credit risks.

Sample copies. Every advertiser should receive a copy of the newspaper in which his ad appears, each time it appears. Some will also request *tear sheets* —clippings of the page on which the ad appears—to be sent with the bill, especially if they share advertising costs with a manufacturer.

Classified ads. A good classified ad section can work wonders for your circulation figures. For this reason (and because we think there are too few real bargains around these days), our policy is to charge only a token amount for classified ads; it creates good will and reader interest that cannot be measured in dollars. Businesses that take out classified ads must pay in advance, and we charge them a higher rate. Here is the policy we print in our classifed ad section:

> As a public service, the Harvard Post will print free of charge any ad offering to share something with the community (e.g., rides, child care, free items). In addition, there is no charge for Lost and Found, or for ads placed by students seeking work.
>
> All other ads will be published in two consecutive issues for a flat fee of one dollar. We must limit ads to 50 words. This policy does not apply to ads placed by businesses, which cost $4 per week, payable in advance. The editors reserve the right to edit or reject any ad.
>
> Send ads to the Harvard Post, Box 308, Harvard, Mass. 01451, or call GL 6-8122 before 12 noon Tuesday. Please send payment (postage stamps or cash preferred) with your ad. The Honor System will apply; we do not send bills.

Do people take advantage of our "Honor System" by not paying for their ads? We don't really know, because we don't keep records. As far as we're concerned, the system works beautifully: our classified pages are packed with interesting ads, there is no bookkeeping involved, our readers can't wait to see the paper each week, and people are always stopping us on the street to give us money.

WHAT THE AD REP SHOULD REMEMBER

Know the product you're selling. Merchants will be interested in circulation figures, including what percentage of your community reads the newspaper; demographic information, such as how much the average reader earns per year (check with the U.S. Bureau of the Census or the local Board of Realtors for this kind of information); and any special characteristics of the paper that you might point out (strong emphasis on environmental issues, the arts, or the like).

Get to know the client you're selling to. Check out the store as soon as you walk in, for the kind of goods it sells, for any merchandise marked "special" or "sale," for imaginative display devices that might be converted to good ads. Mention these to the merchant as possibilities for ads. *Be specific.* An ad that shows one piece of merchandise, with a catchy lead-in, a short description, and a price, will do more to draw in customers than four ads with the words "best selection in the area."

Weed out unfriendly or definitely uninterested customers by your judicious use of the telephone before you go out pounding the pavement. Don't ask on the phone, "Would you like an ad this week?" Say, "I was planning to stop by to see you about an ad. Is that convenient for you?" If they turn you off at that point, it's not worth stopping. Even if a customer turns you down flat, though, woo him or her with an occasional visit.

Give or send sample copies of the paper to ad prospects, together with a rate card. Let them know that you're sending it by a phone call, and visit them shortly afterwards to talk over advertising possibilities.

Keep a record of when advertisers indicate they might be interested in an ad. (Never forget to ask, "When should I call on you again?" if they turn you down.) If you call on them when they've suggested, they'll appreciate your reminder.

Regular smaller ads are apt to get better results for the merchant than occasional larger ones. Suggest a standard format by which the advertiser can create an image. Then insert specific merchandise into the format as frequently as possible. An effective, memorable ad that will save everyone time and work will be the result.

Don't take for granted regular advertisers—the ones who run the same spot ad every week. Drop in on them every once in a while to see if they'd like a change or a few extra copies of any issue.

Take advantage of holidays and seasonal changes to encourage the appropriate merchants to advertise. Again, be specific. Suggest to that shoe store that back-to-school time is when it might best advertise its special on children's shoes.

Comb through rival publications to find ads that would be suitable for use in your paper. It's perfectly all right to call a merchant and say, "I saw your ad in last week's Gazette. We could run the same ad for $8.50 in this Friday's Post. Would you like to try it?" Whether or not you reset the type, you've saved time and effort; and very often you can win the advertiser's good will by making a better-looking ad out of the very same copy. *Note:* Don't be miffed if you see one of your ads in someone else's paper. It's a compliment to your accomplishment. In any case, advertising matter isn't copyrighted along with the editorial content of your newspaper, unless you specify that artwork created by your staff is so protected.

Merchants who are skeptical of the drawing power of their newspaper advertising should know that business will prosper only if customers are reminded that their services exist. Effective weekly advertising is like having a good salesperson in the community, hustling up business and returning a good profit on the amount invested. Don't be discouraged; it takes persistent, intelligent communication with the reluctant merchant to convince him or her that advertising pays off. And get friends who support the paper to mention it in the stores they visit—if customers speak of the ads, or the lack of them, a storekeeper will feel more willing. The lack of people mentioning a store's advertising, though, shouldn't be used by the merchant as a justification for not placing ads; most people just don't converse that easily about their motives for making a purchase.

Making up the ad. Writing good ad copy that accurately yet imaginatively reflects the style and products of a business is an invaluable skill; study effective ads wherever you notice them to analyze how it's done. If you can suggest an eye-catching, tasteful ad to a busy merchant, he or she will be grateful for the help and will often reward you with his advertising patronage. For an especially difficult prospect, it's often worth your while to have the proposed ad set into type and laid out in finished form. When the shopkeeper sees how nice it can look, he or she will often approve it with few changes. *Caution:* Gear the size of the ad as well as its tone to the nature of the establishment. Don't prepare a half-page ad for a little shop; shoot for the possible.

Don't try to cram too much copy, or too many gimmicks, into an ad. One that effectively uses white space will attract much more notice than one that squeezes in every possible bit of copy. A good picture, an eye-catching leading phrase in larger type, a brief description of the merchandise pictured, and a familiar logo for the name and address of the business will do more for the drawing power of an ad than a busy and cramped listing of ten times as many items.

It always helps to have a good artist on the staff for adding special touches to mundane ads. Whether or not you do, though, you should make use of already available commercial art to dress up your ads. There are many inexpensive books of copyright-free "clip art" for the graphic artist; the best are published by Dover Publications, Inc. (180 Varick Street, New York, N.Y. 10014). Also, there are more expensive services—such as the Metro Newspaper Service (80 Madison Avenue, New York, N.Y. 10016)— that will send you every month a big book full of advertising art ready to be clipped out and pasted in. Most of the art is fairly tacky, but for a Christmas wreath or a Halloween pumpkin it's just fine. (Note: Any photographs provided by these art services are prescreened; you can see the screen if you look carefully. You therefore don't need to set them aside for the printer to shoot separately. See *Printing,* pages 37–39.)

Evaluate the material that an advertiser gives you to see if it will reproduce well. The ad representative should spend at least some time in the layout room, in order to understand better the problems of enlarging, reducing, and reproducing copy; but here are a few things to watch for:

¶ Accept ads clipped from other newspapers only with the reminder that they may have to be reset in order to get clean, attractive copy. If you have a photostat camera, it may be possible for their quality to be brought up a peg or two by dropping out dirty-looking backgrounds; otherwise, it might be worth asking your printer to shoot the ad separately, supplying a blackout in its place on the layout sheets.

¶ Don't try to use photographs clipped from other newspapers' ads; they've already been screened and printed once, and will suffer terribly if you screen and print them again.

¶ Color pictures also reproduce poorly. Warn the advertiser.

¶ Any material printed in light blue, violet, light grey, yellow, or other light colors will not reproduce. If the advertiser doesn't want this material reset, ask for it in black, red, or orange.

The advertising in a newspaper, both in its content and its graphic quality, should reflect the good taste and the quality of the publication. This means that the publisher not only has the responsibility to reject misleading ads, but also has the right to reject ads that are in poor taste. It is proper for a publisher to turn down:

¶ ads with a lot of heavy or oversized black lettering;

¶ reversed ads (white lettering on a black background) of more than a certain size. We feel that a quarter page is the absolute

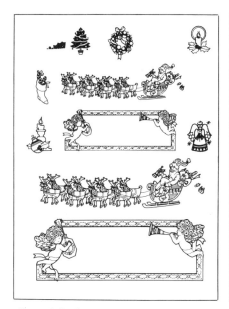

Copyright-free "clip art."

maximum for reversed ads in a small-format newspaper; the reverses require heavy inking that adversely affects photographs printed on the same page, and they get readers' fingers dirty as well. Suggest that such ads be screened to a certain percentage of black—perhaps 60 or 70 percent—so that they will appear as grey instead of black and thus be toned down;

¶ upside-down ads;

¶ crudely hand-lettered ads;

¶ screamingly brassy ads.

Ad mock-ups. For each new ad and each ad with a copy change, the advertising representative should draw a mock-up. On a fresh sheet of paper, draw the outline of the ad in the exact size it is to appear in print. (We have forms printed up in advance with one-, two-, and three-column blocks up to nine inches high, with dotted lines indicating height at one-inch increments.) Then write inside the block *all* the copy that belongs in the ad—giving appropriate emphasis where desired. If there is an illustration, attach it to the sheet with a paper clip, and make a rough sketch in the ad block. This gives the advertising production manager a clear idea of how the ad is supposed to look (which will be very helpful when specifying type.) And it helps the ad rep realize before deadline time if the desired copy just isn't going to fit in the space purchased.

Advertising checklist. Each week, when all the ads have been assembled, each advertising representative should prepare a complete list of his or her

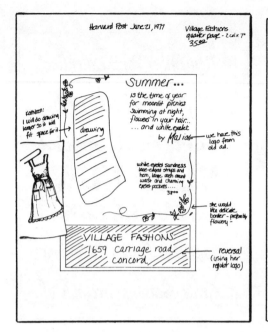

Left, an ad mock-up, prepared by the ad representative and supplying all the information needed for specifying type and laying out the ad. At right, an advertising checklist.

ads for that issue. A separate "house list" should be prepared by the business manager for ads that came in unsolicited, unless there is an agreement that the advertising manager is given commissions on such ads as well. The advertising checklist should include:

¶ a heading showing the issue's date and the name of the salesperson;

¶ the name of each advertiser (including billing information for new accounts);

¶ the size of each ad;

¶ the price of each ad;

¶ the total advertising dollars for that issue.

This list should be used during layout for checking that all ads have been included in the paper; and it will be used later by the bookkeeper for keeping records of ad payments, commissions, and so forth. (See *Financial Matters,* pages 153–154.) Keep old checklists in a special file.

If you have access to a small computer, you will want to keep your advertising records on it. Because we found that commercially available software did not meet the special needs of newspaper advertising—discount schedules, commissions, billing, cross-referenced checklists, and the like— we have had a special program written for this purpose; for more information write to us at P.O. Box 308, Harvard, Mass. 01451.

9 Circulation and Distribution

IF YOU ARE STARTING A SMALL NEWSPAPER, certain decisions having to do with its distribution will have to be made right at the beginning. Among these are:

¶ Will it be distributed free or will people have to pay for it?

¶ If the latter, what will its subscription and newsstand prices be?

¶ What will the publication schedule be? That is, if it is to be a weekly, on what day of the week will it appear?

¶ How will it be distributed? By mail (regular second-class, second-class controlled circulation, or third-class), by newsstand sales or street hawkers, by home delivery, or by having readers pick up free copies at stores and other public places?

¶ If it is a paid-circulation newspaper, how are you going to get people to subscribe to it, or notice it on a crowded newsstand?

Free or paid circulation? There are arguments to be made on both sides of this question, but we feel very strongly that any newspaper worth reading is worth paying for. A free-distribution paper, no matter how good it is, runs the risk of being classified out of hand as "junk mail," and as such will be automatically tossed into the wastebasket by a lot of people. On the other hand, a well-written, cleanly designed, and community-conscious newspaper will find that a large percentage of its potential readers are quite willing to pay for it—as indeed they should be.

Moreover, there are several distinct advantages to the paid-circulation choice. First, there is the income that you will realize from subscriptions and newsstand sales. It will not be the largest portion of your revenue; most paid-circulation newspapers derive 70 to 80 percent of their gross income from advertising. But it will help. Second, paid-circulation publications can qualify for lower postal rates—another important financial consideration. (See page 118 for a discussion of second-class mailing.) Third, printing and distribution costs will be lower, because you will print and send a copy of the paper not to every household in town but only to the ones that want it. There was a time not too long ago when newsprint was cheap and third-class (junk mail) postage rates were very low. These conditions contributed to the remarkable proliferation of free-distribution papers, flyers, and "advertisers" that threatened to bury the United States Postal Service. But paper, printing, and postage costs all have skyrocketed in the past decade—all good reasons to favor the paid-circulation choice. Fourth, only paid-circulation papers qualify for legal advertising, which can be a significant source of income (see *Advertising,* page 106). And finally, your paper will be accorded a greater degree of respect, by both readers and discriminating advertisers, if it is not a give-away. A paid circulation is the only sure indication of real involvement and interest on the part of the people you are trying to serve.

The main advantage to free distribution is that you can give potential advertisers a nice fat circulation figure and tell them that you have saturated the market—although this is not strictly true, because many people will never even look at a free paper and others will glance through it so quickly that few of the ads will really be noticed. Many advertisers, unfortunately, attach more significance to the circulation figure than to any other factor, and will therefore be tempted by free distribution. Another advantage is the saving in bookkeeping work that comes from not having to bother with a subscription list and all that goes with it—record-keeping, renewal notices, addressing problems, and so on. But this should not be considered a major deterrent, and we will show you later in this chapter how to deal with subscriptions in a fairly painless way.

Let us assume, then, that you have followed our advice and decided to make your readers pay for their newspaper.

Setting the price. This will depend partly on your projected operating costs, partly on your competition, and partly on what you think the market will bear. If your newspaper is intended primarily for working-class people, the elderly, or any other group that is likely to have limited resources, you must set the price at a level that they would find reasonable. If you are going to publish a biweekly newsletter for doctors, however, go ahead and charge them an arm and a leg, so to speak.

If you are starting up a small community paper and you are competing with a large area weekly that charges $7.50 for a year's subscription, don't set your subscription price higher. It may be advantageous to underprice your paper—at first, at least. You can always raise the price later, after readers have grown attached to the new publication. If the prospects for attracting advertisers don't seem good, you may have to set your subscription price high and plan to derive a greater than usual percentage of your income from newspaper sales rather than advertising. (If prospects for advertising look really bad, you are probably getting yourself into big trouble.) The more specialized the subject of your publication, the more money people will be willing to pay for it. Few small-community newspapers charge more than $12 or at most $15 for a year's subscription, but many specialized trade journals and newsletters cost a great deal more than that. In general, we feel that the price of the newspaper should correspond to what you yourself would be comfortable paying for it. When we started the Harvard Post in 1973 we charged ten cents a copy on the newsstands and $5 a year for subscriptions because that seemed like the proper price for a skinny little small-town paper. Ten years later it is a quarter on the stands and $10 for a year's subscription.

The subscription price should reflect a discount over the total newsstand price for a year's worth of issues. This will provide some incentive for readers to subscribe. You may want to offer further discounts on two- or three-year subscriptions, since they will save you a certain amount of bookkeeping work. You may also decide to charge a higher rate for out-of-county, out-of-state, or foreign subscriptions, because of the additional mailing costs (see below). We offer special nine-month subscriptions, designed for students who are living away from home, at a discount rate. Other possible discounts might be established for elderly subscribers, or for people who purchase multiple gift subscriptions.

Day of publication. The most common day of the week by far for publication of weekly community newspapers is Thursday. The runners-up seem to be Wednesday and Friday. The reason for this is that many advertisers prefer to have their ads come out around the middle of the week —just as the heaviest shopping days are starting. This is especially true of supermarkets and other stores that have weekly specials or sales. Midweek publication is not always the best plan from the standpoint of covering the news, though. If the town council or the school committee meets on Tuesday night, for example, you would be able to get the news of their meetings into a Friday newspaper the same week, whereas a Thursday paper would most likely have to wait until the news was a week old.

The one crucial consideration is your printer. You will be lucky indeed if the printer who gives you the lowest bid is also able to put your paper on the press when you want him to. In short, you will have to balance a number of conflicting factors in deciding on a day: your printer's schedule, the expected flow of news, and the wishes of advertisers. If there is a local supermarket owner who could be persuaded to take a regular large ad on condition that you publish on Wednesday, that might in itself be reason enough to do it.

The date on the newspaper should correspond to the day that most local readers receive it. Some newspapers use a later date, to make each issue seem more current even after it is a few days old—a needlessly confusing practice, in our view.

Second-class mailing. Getting a second-class mailing permit will almost certainly be the most economical way to distribute your newspaper, especially if it is a small one. This is because second-class rates are based on the weight of the newspaper, as well as on the distance it must be mailed. The lowest rate is for copies sent within the same county as the place of publication: the current charge (as of May 1983) is 4.1 cents per pound, plus 2.6 cents per piece. The per-piece charge goes down to 2.1 cents for copies that are sorted and bundled according to mail carrier routes. This means that a compact-size paper of, say, twelve or sixteen pages can be mailed within a county for less than 2½ cents.

The pound rate increases rapidly as the distance to be mailed goes up. Also, the cost of outside-the-county mailing is computed according to a complicated system in which the charge increases proportionally with the percentage of advertising in the issue. Furthermore, the per-piece charge for out-of-county mailing depends on the total number of copies to be mailed: publications mailing 5,000 or more out of the county are charged 4.4 to 7 cents per piece (depending on how they are sorted), whereas those mailing fewer than 5,000 pay 3 to 5.1 cents. (The per-piece charge is always additional to the pound rate.) Thus, a small paper with fewer than 5,000 out-of-county subscribers and, say, 50 percent advertising can be sent across the country for 5 to 7½ cents. With more than 5,000 out-of-county, the charge is 7 to 9½ cents. There are also special lower rates for publications of nonprofit organizations and societies; for religious, educational, and scientific publications designed for classroom use; and for publications "designed to promote the science of agriculture."

Clearly, the second-class postage rates have been set up to favor small, local publications, and this remains true despite the recent series of very large across-the-board postage rate increases. Large-circulation newspapers and magazines—particularly those with nationwide readership—have been hit hard by these rate hikes. Small-town newspapers have been hurt as well, but they continue to enjoy much lower postage rates.

The most important person in all your dealings with the post office is the local postmaster. If you have not already struck up a friendship with him or her, do so at once. The postmaster's good will and cooperation will mean the difference between painlessness and real agony as you wade through federal regulations, permit applications, and an almost hopeless confusion of Postal Service forms. If you live in a small town, yours may be the first application for a second-class permit that the local postmaster has had to deal with. If so, get hold of the appropriate government documents and forms (start with Publication 114, "Second-Class Mailings"), sit down with the postmaster, and go over them together until you are sure that you both understand them. You are bound to make some mistakes along the way; but with the postmaster on your side, and with any luck, nothing horrible will happen.

In order to qualify for second-class privileges a publication must be issued regularly, at least four times a year, according to a stated schedule. It must have a legitimate list of paid subscribers; free-circulation papers may not qualify. The amount of space devoted to advertising may not exceed 75 percent in more than half of the issues during any twelve-month period. ("Advertising," according to the Postal Service, includes all space that has been paid for, whether it appears as an ad or as a "news article"; it also includes any of the publisher's own ads, even though they are not, of course, paid for.) These are just a few of the applicable restrictions. Check the postal regulations for a complete list.

After you have applied for your second-class permit and paid the required $160 fee, you must wait for the application to be approved by the director of mail classification in Washington, D.C. There is no way to predict how long this will take; it could be two weeks or two years. The postal authorities have been known to take inordinate amounts of time to approve second-class applications from left-wing or radical periodicals. They may request additional sample issues for inspection, or other information not included in your original application.

What do you do while waiting for the second-class permit to be approved? It is essential that you send out the papers at third-class postage rates during this waiting period: postal regulations provide that the difference between the third- and second-class rates may be refunded to you on all such mailings once the second-class permit is approved, *but only if the local postmaster has kept a record of the third-class mailings on Postal Form 3503.* The third-class mailing will cost you dearly—the 1983 rates are 7.4 to 11 cents per piece, depending on how they are sorted—but at least you will get most of it back eventually. You will get no refund, however, if Form 3503 is not kept or if you send out papers with postage stamps affixed.

SIDE A (For Regular Rate Publications)	U.S. Postal Service — STATEMENT OF MAILING—2nd-CLASS PUBS EXCEPT REQUESTER PUBLICATIONS (See DMM 482)

PUBLICATION NO. 9 9 1 8 2 0

NAME OF PUBLICATION OR NEWS AGENT: THE HARVARD POST

DATE OF MAILING: (Mo.) 4 (Day) 1 4 (Yr.) 8 3

POST OFFICE AND STATE: HARVARD, MASS.

ZIP CODE: 0 1 4 5 1 - 0 3 0 8

FINANCE NUMBER: 2 4 - 3 2 98

When this statement is for ALL ISSUES for a calendar month, multiply the number of addressed pieces per issue by the No. of issues and put the result in the appropriate blocks of items 5, 6, 8, and 9. Also furnish the following information:
NUMBER OF ISSUES: _____
WEIGHT OF ONE SHEET (482.34 __ __ . __ __ __ __ __ __ LBS.)
COMBINED WEIGHT OF ONE COPY FROM EACH ISSUE __ __ . __ __ __ __ __ LBS.

DATE OF ISSUE PRINTED IN COPIES: 4/15/83

FREQUENCY OF ISSUE: WEEKLY

AVERAGE WEIGHT PER COPY FOR THE ISSUE (482.23): _ _ . 1 2 4 3 7 5 LBS.

When postage is computed at the key rate, the lines for Zones 1 to 8 need not be completed for each issue. The total zone mailings must be entered in item 1 during the time the key rate is in effect.

Incidental 1st-Class Attached or Enclosed ☐ Yes ☐ No

EDITION CODE OR KEY: 48

STATEMENT NO. (In sequence):

FREIGHT BILL NO.:

POST OFFICE COMPUTED AVERAGE OR COMBINED WEIGHT PER COPY: _ _ . 1 2 4 3 7 5 LBS.

POUND RATE — OUTSIDE COUNTY

1. Advertising Portion PERCENTAGE FOR: ONE ISSUE OR ALL ISSUES for a calendar month

ZONE	A *NON-SUBSCRIBERS' COPIES	B SUBSCRIBERS' COPIES	C TOTAL COPIES	D TOTAL (Pounds)	E ADVERTISING PORTION (Pounds)	F. POSTAGE RATE PER POUND OR FRACTION — Regular	G COMPUTED POSTAGE
1 AND 2	35	273	308	39	19	17.1¢	3.25
3		45	45	6	3	18.4¢	.56
4		54	54	7	3	20.8¢	.63
5		46	46	6	3	24.6¢	.74
6		33	33	5	3	29.1¢	.88
7		46	46	6	3	33.4¢	1.01
8		43	43	6	3	38.3¢	1.15
TOTAL COPIES	35	540	575	75	37	**Total advertising postage**	8.22

2. TOTAL POUNDS ALL ZONES — 75 / 37

3. Total advertising portion (Col. E line 2) — 37 ▲ Key rate, if used ▲

4. Nonadvertising Portion (Col. D line 2 minus line 3) — 38 — 12.8¢ — 4.87

PER PIECE CHARGES (in addition to the pound rate)

5. ☐ REGULAR RATE OR ☐ SCIENCE OF AGRICULTURE
For mailings of 5,000 or more copies per issue outside county

LEVEL		Total Copies	No. of Addressed Pieces	Rate		
A. Copies not meeting requirements for level B or C rate.				7.0¢		
B. Packages of six or more addressed pieces labeled and sacked to 5-digit, 3-digit city or optional city destinations (see 467.6, DMM)				5.4¢		
C. Packages of six or more addressed pieces labeled and sacked to carrier route or carrier routes destinations (see 467.6, DMM)				4.4¢		

6. ☒ Ltd. Circ. Rate ☐ Ltd. Circ. Science of Agric. Rate
Mailings under 5,000 copies per issue outside county

LEVEL		Total Copies	No. of Addressed Pieces	Rate		
D. Copies not meeting requirements for level E or F rate.		446		5.1¢		22.75
E. Packages of six or more addressed pieces labeled and sacked to 5-digit, 3-digit city or optional city destinations (see 467.6, DMM)		129		3.5¢		4.52
F. Packages of six or more addressed pieces labeled and sacked to carrier route or carrier routes destinations (see 467.6, DMM)				3.0¢		

7. POUND RATE — Nonsubscriber Copies 30 — Subscriber Copies 989 — Total Copies 1019 — Total Pounds 127 — 4.1¢ — 5.21

IN-COUNTY

8. PER PIECE CHARGES (In addition to the pound rate.)

LEVEL		Total Copies	No. of Addressed Pieces	Rate		
J. Copies not meeting requirements for level K rate.			1019	2.6¢		26.50
K. Packages of six or more addressed pieces labeled and sacked to carrier route or carrier routes destinations (see 467.6, DMM)				2.1¢		

9. FOREIGN (Publishers Periodicals) WEIGHT PER COPY (must include the wrapping) — Nonsubscriber Copies — Subscriber Copies 20 — Total Copies 20 — Rate Per Copy .17 — 3.40

10. NONSUBSCRIBER COPIES
Complete Form 3541-A for commingled nonsubscriber copies which exceed the 10% allowance in 426.1, DMM and attach to this Form.
Compute postage on attached Form 3541-A and write postage amount in Col. G of this line for nonsubscriber copies in excess of 10% limit. ➤

11. MAILED BY (Signature required) — TELEPHONE NO. 456-8122

12. COMPUTED BY (Signature required)

TOTAL POSTAGE CHARGE: 75.47

*Only commingled nonsubscriber copies within the 10% limitation of 426.1, DMM are to be shown in items 1 thru 9 of this form. Postage for other commingled nonsubscriber copies is to be reported on Form 3541-A. Nonsubscriber copies which are not commingled with subscriber copies are subject to the transient rate. (Mailer must fill in unshaded blocks)

PS Form 3541, Dec. 1982

FINANCIAL DOCUMENT – FORWARD TO FINANCE OFFICER

A completed post office statement of mailing for second-class publications. The information in the shaded areas is filled in by the local postmaster.

Third-class postage should be paid directly to the post office, and a notice reading "Third-class postage paid at (city), (state)" should be printed on the front of the paper.

Postal regulations for second-class mail require that the name of the publication "be shown on the front or cover page in a position and in a style and size of type that makes it clearly distinguishable from the name of the publisher or other items on the front." The following information must also be printed in each issue on one of the first five pages, or in the masthead on the editorial page:

¶ The name of the publication and its publication number (supplied by the Postal Service).

¶ The date of issue.

¶ The statement of frequency of publication.

¶ The issue number (each successive issue must be numbered consecutively).

¶ The subscription price.

¶ The address of the known office of publication, including zip code.

¶ The second-class indicia, reading "Second-class postage paid at (town), (state), (zip code)." When a publication is mailed at two or more offices, the indicia must read "Second-class postage paid at (town), (state), (zip code) and at additional mailing offices." When copies are mailed while an application is pending, the notice should read "Application to mail at second-class postage rates is pending at (town), (state, zip code)."

¶ An address to which subscribers and postal officials can write to request changes of address.

After your second-class permit has been approved you will have to fill out a statement of mailing for each issue; the postmaster will use this form to compute the proper postage charge. You will have to include the average weight per copy of the issue (worked out to six decimal places), the percentage of advertising in the issue, and the number of subscribers' copies and sample (free) copies sent to each postal zone. The statement of mailing must be accompanied by a "checking copy" of the newspaper, on which you have clearly marked all the advertising portions. Your postmaster will help you figure all this out.

You must also file by October 1 of each year a statement of ownership, management, and circulation. The information called for on this statement

—the names of the newspaper's owners, publishers, and editors; their addresses; circulation figures broken down into the numbers of paid and free copies; and so forth—must also be printed in the newspaper itself, and its accuracy must be sworn to by the person filing the statement.

How reliable is second-class mailing? It varies. Papers sent to nearby areas usually are delivered promptly. Those that must travel greater distances are often subject to unaccountable hazards and delays. Dated material such as weekly newspapers is supposed to be given high-priority treatment by the post office, but this is not always done. Subscribers who experience delivery problems should be encouraged to talk to their local postal workers; often, once the mail carrier knows that you're looking for your favorite small newspaper to be on time, he or she will make a special effort to get it to you.

Controlled-circulation mailing. There is a special category of second-class mailing called controlled-circulation or "requester" publication rates. These are higher than regular second-class rates, but lower than third-class. They are intended for publications that do not have paid circulations but are more than just advertising sheets. To qualify for these rates a publication must have at least 24 pages, must contain at least 25 percent nonadvertising matter, must be issued at regular intervals at least four times a year, and must not be owned or controlled by an individual or business that publishes it mainly for business purposes. (For example, a newspaper published by a corporation mainly for the purpose of advertising its services would not qualify for controlled-circulation mailing.) The publication must also have a legitimate list of persons who have asked to receive it, and at least half the copies must be distributed to persons who have made such requests. See your postmaster for other regulations and restrictions that apply to these mailings.

Third-class mailing. Though third-class mail rates are generally higher than second-class, there are some circumstances in which third-class mailing is a good choice. For instance, the special third-class rates for nonprofit organizations are among the lowest of all postage rates. Also, third-class rates do not vary with the distance to be covered, as second-class rates do. Therefore, the advantage of second-class mailing is less for a publication whose subscribers are widely scattered around the country. In general, though, for the small local newspaper third-class mail should be used only as a temporary measure while a second-class permit is pending.

Newsstand sales. It is important that your new newspaper be available at every newsstand in an area where a significant number of people might be interested in reading it. If yours is a community newspaper, accomplishing this will not be much of a problem. There are not likely to be too many local newsstands, and their proprietors will probably be very happy to sell the paper. You can make the deliveries yourself, picking up any unsold copies of the previous issue and collecting money for those that have been sold. This routine will enable you to enjoy the singular pleasure of finding people waiting at the store for you to arrive so that they can get their newspapers "hot off the press." (Try to establish and maintain a regular schedule for delivery of the papers to the stores; many readers will prefer to buy their copies there every week rather than wait for them to come in the mail next morning, and they want the paper to be there when they go to buy it.)

Talk to the various newsstand owners sometime before your first issue to let them know what you are planning to do and to agree on an appropriate commission. The store should get between 25 and 40 percent of the newsstand price. Newsstand sales are invariably handled on a consignment basis: the store pays only for those copies of the previous issue that have actually been sold. Try to arrange to have your paper displayed in a prominent place, and see if the stand owner will allow you to put up a small but eye-catching sign calling attention to the new publication and exciting the curiosity of potential readers. (See related remarks below about promotion.)

You will need to set up a *circulation record book* in which you note the number of copies of each issue left at every newsstand, the number of unsold copies picked up, and the amount of money collected. These records will allow you to keep track of the pattern of sales at each location, and to determine the number of copies of the next issue that should be delivered. Ideally, each newsstand should sell out its last copy of the paper just as the new edition hits the streets.

In the circulation record book you should also enter subscription totals from issue to issue, keeping a running account of the number of new subscribers and the number of cancellations. The book will thus contain a continuous record of your paid circulation. If you enjoy visual displays, you can make a large graph of this data, with issue dates on the horizontal axis and circulation figures on the vertical, and hang it over your desk.

If your potential readers are spread out over a large area— for example, if you are starting a newspaper for Volkswagen owners in the state of Texas—newsstand sales may not be feasible. You could try, though, to get news distributors to carry your paper. Such distributors, usually found in every large and medium-size city, buy quantities of many periodicals directly from the publishers at wholesale prices, and then supply them to the various stores and newsstands in their areas. Distributors are usually extremely reluctant to take on a new small publication. Specific requests from newsstand owners will help.

If your newspaper is competing for space at crowded newsstands with dozens or even hundreds of other publications, pay special attention to your front-page design and headlines. Do everything possible to make the paper attractive, eye-catching, irresistible. In other words, be bold.

Street hawkers. The street-hawker system has been used successfully by many urban alternative small newspapers; it is well suited to compact-size papers in densely populated areas. Bundles of papers are distributed at central locations to the hawkers, who come at a set time each week. The hawkers must pay for the papers they take, at the wholesale rate, at the time of pickup. Then they are free to sell them wherever they can, simply pocketing the proceeds. Usually each hawker will have a favorite street corner or neighborhood that is considered his or her territory. Unsold papers may be returned for credit the following week.

Home delivery. For a small, paid-circulation newspaper, there is little likelihood that home delivery by carriers will compare favorably with second-class mail delivery. But many free publications have recently changed from third-class or controlled-circulation mailing to a home-delivery system because of increased postage rates. Carriers are hired to leave a copy of the paper at every house in an area. Often the papers are put in plastic bags and hung on doorknobs or, in rural areas, on mailbox posts. Postal regulations prohibit the placing of such items in the mailboxes themselves. Residents sometimes complain about such deliveries, both because of the tendency of the plastic bags and their contents to litter the neighborhood and because an uncollected bag can tip off a would-be burglar about a temporarily unoccupied home.

Centralized free distribution. One way to distribute a free newspaper is simply to leave piles of copies in public places where people can pick them up. Here again, an attractive front page is important.

PROMOTION TECHNIQUES—HOW TO GET SUBSCRIBERS

Ultimately, the best way to get people to subscribe to your newspaper is to make it as informative, entertaining, and attractive as possible. This means clean design and layout, accurate and aggressive reporting, good writing and scrupulous editing. No amount of promotion gimmicks can substitute for these essentials.

But people must have a chance to see and read your paper before they can decide to subscribe to it. Especially with a new publication, your initial promotion campaign can mean the difference between a healthy start and a long struggle. The accepted way to begin such a campaign is with at least one and often several complimentary issues that are sent out, by means of a free mailing, to the whole town (or whatever community of people you intend to serve).

Preparing the first issue. The quality of your first issue is crucial, for it will create an impression that will be hard to alter. Plan your news stories, features, editorials, and illustrations with this in mind. Even if you have no idea what you're going to do for the second issue, make the first one a knockout. (When we put together the first issue of the Harvard Post in 1973 we didn't even have plans to put out a second one. But a hundred families— 10 percent of the town—liked that first Post enough to send in their subscription checks right away, and that alone gave us the desire to continue.)

Because you are going to send a complimentary copy to every household, you should have no trouble getting advertisers for the first issue. In fact, some merchants may be offended if you neglect to ask them for an ad. This is your chance to visit each of the town's leading citizens—bankers, businesspeople, public officials—and tell them of your plans. Many of them will have advice for you; much more important than their advice, however, is the interest and anticipation that will be generated by your making the rounds in this way. The birth of a newspaper is a historic occasion. Treat it as one.

Whatever else goes into your introductory issues, two things are essential: you must make it very clear to your readers how many free issues they can expect to receive and at what point they must subscribe in order to continue getting the paper; and you must make the subscription process itself as simple and obvious as possible. A large subscription ad with a coupon to be cut out and sent in is probably the best way. Put it in a very prominent position—the back page is ideal. (Don't give in to the temptation to put your subscription ad on the front page; that precious space should be reserved for the news and other information that is your paper's primary reason for existence. Instead, put a small news story in a box on the front page announcing the advent of the newspaper, the initial publication schedule of complimentary issues, and the fact that a subscription coupon may be found on the back page.)

The free mailing. Talk to your postmaster about the mechanics of sending out a complimentary issue by third-class mail. Find out how the papers should be bundled to make it easiest on the mail carriers, as this will qualify you for the lowest postage rate. See the remarks above about getting a partial refund on the third-class postage after your second-class permit has been approved. The postal regulations allow you to send out free copies up to a limit of 10 percent of the total number of copies mailed in a year. Above the 10 percent limit free copies must be mailed at a higher rate.

At the same time that you are sending out complimentary issues, place stacks of newspapers in supermarkets, drug stores, newsstands, and other spots where curious people may pick them up and take them home. Make sure the public library has several copies of each issue. Try to saturate the community during those first crucial weeks to make sure that everyone is saying, "Have you seen the new newspaper yet?"

If the community to which you want to send your free copies is not a town but, rather, a more diverse and scattered group, the promotional mailing will be a bit more complicated. You will have to compile a mailing list of good prospects and then address each of the newspapers one by one. Mailing lists can be obtained from many sources, including other publications, directories of various kinds, professional organizations, the government, and commercial mailing-list dealers. Some companies will give away or sell lists of their customers. A great deal of information can be obtained from the library by checking reference books. Once you have made a mailing to a particular list of people, keep careful records of the resulting response. A successful direct-mail campaign is thought to be one that produces a 3-percent or greater response. Most good lists will be worth using several times; one that gets a 5-percent response to the first mailing may well get another 4 percent on the second. (Of course, you must "clean" the list by removing from it the names of people who have already responded.) Keep using the list until the response is below 3 percent.

Follow-up techniques. A tedious but effective way to follow up a free mailing is with a telephone campaign. Call each of the people in town, or on your mailing list, ask whether he received his complimentary copy of the newspaper, what he thought of it, and whether he would like to subscribe. Naturally, the person who does this should have a pleasant voice. Use this opportunity for personal intercourse to get ideas and suggestions on how to improve the paper. Someone might say, "I'll subscribe to your newspaper if you print the news of the Parcheesi Club." If you can make room for Parcheesi, you will have won at least one reader, and probably the rest of the club members as well.

If the person sounds reluctant on the telephone, offer him a four-week trial subscription. If after four issues he decides he doesn't want the paper, he can cancel without obligation. Otherwise you will bill him for a year's subscription. Four weeks of a really good newspaper can establish a strong habit.

Even after your initial subscription campaign is over use every chance you get to promote the paper and win new readers. Give out sample copies freely to anyone who expresses interest. Provide extra copies to advertisers and to the people you write about. Try to make it a habit to ask people with whom you are speaking whether they get the paper, and if they would like you to enter a subscription for them. Put up signs at newsstands, if the owners will let you. Offer to speak for free to civic groups, fraternal organizations, and schools about your new venture. Paint the name of your newspaper on the side of your car. The best follow-up technique of all is to fill the paper with original material of genuine interest to the community.

Designing ads for yourself. Try to make room for a subscription ad and coupon in almost every issue. It needn't be large, but it should be easy to find and clip out. It can be very helpful in layout to have made up in advance several subscription ads of different sizes, and to be able to fill out a page with one in just the right way. Even a two-inch spot ad saying simply "Subscribe Today!" is better than an empty hole in the page.

Be imaginative. Try to make your own ad the most attractive one in the whole issue. Tell people why they ought to read your newspaper, how it can benefit them, what you plan to do in the next issue. Get permission to use in an ad the lovely note that old Mrs. Mandelbaum sent you with her subscription check. Get a picture of Mrs. Mandelbaum to go with it. Make up a variety of ads that will appeal to different kinds of people, and alternate them from issue to issue. Sell gift subscriptions in December; sell student subscriptions for the college kids going away in September.

Periodic subscription drives. Even after your publication is established you can continue to augment your circulation by occasionally sending out another free mailing. Pick a special issue that you know is going to be of intense interest to your readers and blanket the community again, following up if you can with a telephone campaign. The people who haven't looked at your paper in a while will be impressed at how you've grown and improved. And some people just won't subscribe to a new newspaper until it's been around for a time. After all, they don't want to invest their money in a venture that's going to fold after two months.

HANDLING SUBSCRIPTION RECORDS

One of the first things you will have to do in starting a paid-circulation newspaper is to set up a convenient and simple subscription file. If you are completely unfamiliar with bookkeeping and recordkeeping practices, you will do well to talk to an accountant or some other knowledgeable person about the best way to do these things. This is especially true for setting up the overall financial records of your newspaper (see *Financial Matters,* pages 142–157.)

If you have a microcomputer, you might want to avail yourself here of the portion of our computer program that is set up to take care of subscription records and renewals. (See page 142 for more information.) But a simple file box and a pack of index cards will suffice for your subscription file. A *subscription record card* can be easily designed to suit your particular needs (see example) and you can, if desired, take such a form to your local quick-printing store and have a good supply of cards printed up on index stock. The sample form contains space for the subscriber's name and address, the date the subscription starts (and the date of billing if it is not prepaid), the dates of any renewal notices sent and payments received, the current expiration date, and notations relating to gift subscriptions (see below).

Postal regulations for second-class mail require that accurate records be kept of all subscription payments. If the postal inspectors come to call on you they will demand proof that your subscriptions are actually paid for; this means that the dates of all payments and the expiration dates must be clearly noted on the cards. Moreover, each payment should be carefully entered with the subscriber's name in your general ledger (see additional remarks on this subject in *Financial Matters,* page 144). If you cannot satisfy the inspectors' demands, they have the power to revoke your second-class permit and to make you pay retroactive postage charges at much higher rates—a disaster to be avoided at all costs.

SUBSCRIPTION RECORD	Start:_____ Billed:_____		
Name:_____			
Address:_____	Notices	Paid	Expires
_____			
_____			
Gift of:_____			
Send renewal to:_____			

Keep all of your subscription record cards up to date and in alphabetical order in the file. We find it useful to have two separate files—one for in-town subscribers only, and the other for all out-of-towners. You may wish to further divide your files into geographical areas in order to make it easier to keep tabs on the number of subscriptions in each postal zone. You could have the record cards printed up on stock of different colors to help keep things straight. Don't let yourself fall behind in your recordkeeping work; make out cards for new subscriptions as soon as you get them, make address changes promptly, and when a subscription is cancelled mark the card and take it out of the file, but don't throw it away. Keep it in a special file for possible future reference.

Renewals. As your newspaper approaches its first birthday, you will have another task to carry out. Once a month you should go through the subscription file pulling out the ones that expire during the coming month. (The reason for having the expiration date on the far-right-hand side of the card is to make this job easier.) In preparation for this you should have designed and had printed a subscription renewal notice. Ours is done in the form of a three-by-five index card, which may be easily addressed and mailed as a post card (see example).

Mark the date that the renewal notice was sent on the subscription record card. The number and kind of notices you send your subscribers is up to you. Our preference is not to inundate people with pleas and threats when their subscriptions are running out. We send one regular renewal card during the month preceding the expiration date, and then if the subscriber has neither renewed nor canceled after two or three months have gone by we send one final notice, saying that he has one week in which to respond if he wants his subscription to continue uninterrupted. (See example.) The date of the final notice should be marked on the record card, which is then held out in a special file ready for cancellation after ten days or so have elapsed with no response. You may want to call the subscriber in one final effort to secure the renewal before crossing him off the list; this is a good way to catch those people who can't seem to respond to a written expiration notice.

This general method seems to work extremely well for us. Many people are habitually slow in renewing their subscriptions and will let a month or two go by before remembering to send in a check. But very few fail to respond to the final notice—they realize that they have been delinquent, and, faced with an imminent deadline, they are generally moved to act immediately. Besides the first renewal notice and the final notice, you might also want to have some sort of intermediate notice, perhaps reading: "Have you forgotten? Your subscription has just expired. Renew it today."

There is no point in cutting people's subscriptions off too hastily as a

Dear Subscriber,

Your subscription to the Harvard Post expires on _____.
If you would like us to continue mailing the newspaper to you each
week, please return this card with $10.00 to the Harvard Post, P.O.
Box 308, Harvard, Massachusetts 01451.

We very much appreciate your past support of the Post, and
we look forward to including you in our readership for the coming
year.

_____ Please renew my subscription. I enclose $10.00.
_____ Consider me a Patron of the Post. I enclose _____.
_____ Please cancel my subscription.

Dear Reader,

**Your subscription to the Harvard Post expired on _____.
If you want to continue to receive the newspaper, please send us
$10.00 within the next week. If we don't hear from you in that time,
we will take you off our mailing list.**

The Harvard Post

**The Common
P.O. Box 308
Harvard, MA 01451
(617) 456-8122**

means of getting them to send in renewals; it will just cause you
bookkeeping and addressing headaches and lower your circulation figures
as well. On the other hand, postal regulations do not allow you to carry a
subscription for more than six months after the expiration date and still
count it as part of your paid circulation for second-class mail purposes.

Gift subscriptions. It is a nice touch to have made up a special
announcement card to send recipients of gift subscriptions. (See example.)
They come in handy at Christmastime especially. There should be a spot on
your subscription record card to note the name of the giver if it is a gift
subscription. Also, try to find out who should receive the renewal notice
when the subscription expires, and write this information on the card as
well. We have a special card that we send to the givers of such subscriptions
to encourage them to renew. (See example.)

Sample copies and free subscriptions. You will need to send out a certain number of sample copies of each issue of your newspaper. Each advertiser should receive a free copy so that he can see that his ad actually appeared and check it for errors. You should also send copies to potential advertisers who have expressed interest in seeing what the paper looks like. Send a free copy, as a matter of courtesy, to any nonsubscriber who has provided information or other material that has helped you prepare that issue. All of these must be noted on your statement of mailing as sample copies, not paid circulation.

You will also no doubt want to provide free subscriptions to certain people—relatives, old high-school teachers, old girlfriends or boyfriends, and those people on your Christmas list for whom you can't think of any

---

It is our pleasure to inform you
that you are the recipient of a gift subscription to
The Harvard Post
from

_____

We hope that you enjoy the Post.

Dear _____,
    Your gift subscription to the Post for _____
expires on _____.
    If you would like us to renew this subscription in your name
(please note if you do not want us to send a gift card) just return this
card, with $10.00, to the Harvard Post, The Common, P.O. Box
308, Harvard, Massachusetts 01451.

The Harvard Post

other present. You will be especially tempted to give away a lot of subscriptions when you are just starting the paper and you want to fatten up your circulation. Remember that all such gifts must be counted as sample copies on your mailing statement, and that they are limited to 10 percent of your total circulation. When you do extend a free subscription to someone, make it for a specific period and send him a renewal notice at the end of it. Otherwise you will be continually agonizing over whether or not to cut the person off.

Summary. By following the suggestions above you should be able to set up a subscription file that is efficient and easy to use. The example below shows a typical subscription record as it might appear in your files:

☐ Patron	SUBSCRIPTION RECORD			
			Start: *1/20/81*	
			Billed:	
Name: *Ron + Nancy Reagan*	1st Not.	2nd Not.	Paid	Expires
Address: *The White House*			*$10, 11/7/80*	*1/20/82*
Washington, D.C. 20001	*R-12/15/81*		*$10, 1/14/82*	*1/20/83*
	R-12/17/82	*S-1/15/83*		
		F-4/30/83	*CANCEL —*	*5/14/83*
☒ Gift of: *Y. Andropov*				
Box 57, Moscow, USSR				
Send renewal to: *Reagan*				

This particular subscription was a gift that was paid for on November 7, 1980. The subscription actually started on January 20, 1981. (Note that renewals were to be sent to the recipient of the gift, probably because of the giver's remoteness.) In the "Notices" column, "R" refers to a regular renewal notice, and "F" refers to a final notice. (You could use "S" to signify a second notice, if you use them.) There should be extra room on the record card for noting changes of address.

One final word: A system like this, once it is set up, can be easily used by a bookkeeper or other assistant; the work involved will take up only a few hours each month. But you needn't do things this way at all. There are computer subscription services available that have the whole process automated. Subscribers automatically receive renewal notices and threatening letters, the publisher gets a weekly printout analyzing the newspaper's financial state, and the computer generates address labels, lists of delinquent subscribers, and almost anything else you might want. Such services are expensive. They may save time and effort (although we doubt it), but at what a cost! Computerization, which has so much potential for improving business systems, has all too often instead introduced a faceless, mindless uniformity even in the world of the small independent newspaper —long thought to be a last bastion of individuality and human values. How much more personal it is for your subscribers to receive their renewal notices in your paper's own characteristic style, instead of in the form of the same old trashy computerized message they already get from the telephone company, the electric company, and the bank. Many of your subscribers, when they sit down to write out a renewal check, will take the opportunity to scribble a short note or comment about the paper. How likely are they to do this if the note must be sent not to you but to some computer in the next county? It is these personal communications between a newspaper and its readers that breathe vitality into small-scale journalism. Do away with them at your peril.

More and more now, the computer is not in the next county but in your own office or home. If you have a personal computer, or are considering such an acquisition, see the section on small-newspaper software in the next chapter.

ADDRESSING THE NEWSPAPER

Some newspaper printers have the equipment for printing subscribers' addresses right onto the front of the paper; if your printer can do this at a reasonable cost, and with an error-free system for making corrections and changes, you are in luck. Likewise, if you have been keeping your subscription and advertising records on your own small computer from the start, your task will be made relatively simple; you can have the computer generate address labels in coded categories and you can apply them yourself when the paper comes from the printer. Lacking such alternatives, however, you might be best off at the very start to address your small newspaper by hand. Get a few friends with legible handwriting to come over, make a big batch of popcorn, and have an addressing party, giving each person one section of the subscription file to work on.

Eventually, though, you should reach the point where the hand-addressing system becomes oppressive because of the number of copies to be addressed. There are several other possibilities for mechanized addressing, none of them being completely satisfactory. A mechanical addressing machine, which uses small plates to print the names and addresses onto the papers, will do the job fastest; but such devices, if they are in good condition, cost a great deal of money. In addition, they tend to break down all the time. There are also small hand-held machines that use the spirit-duplication process to print addresses from typed stencils. This process is slow and the stencils begin to fade after not very many weeks of use.

One alternative is to type up a master list of subscribers and then have it printed or photocopied onto adhesive labels. A good photocopying machine will be able to print onto ordinary label sheets—you needn't buy the very expensive sheets made specially for that purpose. The best buy in labels that we've found so far are those made by the Dennison Manufac-turing Company in Framingham, Massachusetts. Before you go ahead and buy twenty boxes of labels, however, make sure that the copying machine you're going to use will accept them. Some sheets tend to slip around in the copier, making the labels come out with the addresses running off the edge. And finally, this is a very difficult system to maintain. It is a real nuisance to add and subtract subscribers from the master list and keep them in any semblance of proper order.

Another alternative is to find someone in your area with a good addressing machine who will allow you to use it on your newspapers once a week for a reasonable fee. Figure out how much the photocopying method above will cost you per label, and compare it with how much it would cost to use someone else's system; then go with whichever is cheaper.

Whatever method you use, make sure that all your new subscriptions, cancellations, and address changes have been duly entered before each issue is addressed for mailing. You may want to set up your list of subscribers for your addressing system in a different order from that used in your subscription file. For example, you can get lower postage rates for second- and third-class mailing by delivering the papers to the post office presorted and bundled into zip-code order and, within each zip code, into individual carrier routes. It will speed the mail delivery as well. Ask your postmaster how he would prefer to have the papers sorted, and do your best to make him happy.

10 Financial Matters

WE HAVE LEARNED A LOT about the business end of the newspaper business in the ten years since we started the Harvard Post. At that time we had not a penny of capital to invest; but we were willing to work hard with little return until the paper got on its feet. By doing everything we possibly could ourselves—writing, editing, advertising sales, typesetting, layout, pasteup, bookkeeping, addressing, and answering the phone—we managed to survive until the Post became firmly entrenched as a town institution with a loyal readership.

Along with a growing readership came increased advertising sales and thus more pages in the Post—which meant that we needed more material; more writers, editors, photographers; and more efficient ways of keeping track of business matters. We still strongly believe that it is possible to start up a newspaper with almost no cash; but having some start-up money available will certainly save you time and effort. Figuring out how much money you will need, and where and how to allocate it, is a complicated process. It involves drawing up a business plan, making financial projections, carrying out market research, calculating the value of an existing newspaper (if you're considering buying one), setting advertising rates, and deciding when to raise them.

Financial planning and basic bookkeeping procedures are the subject of this chapter. But there are many aspects of running a small business that are not covered here; the reader is urged to consult some of the excellent books on the subject. The following discussion is intended as a guide for the inexperienced to setting up the business end of the newspaper in a simple and straightforward way.

PRELIMINARY PLANNING

Buying an existing newspaper. This book is written mostly from the standpoint of someone who wants to start a newspaper from scratch. For a variety of reasons, we believe that starting a paper is usually a better plan than buying one, even if you have substantial capital to invest. But what if you are intent on finding a newspaper to buy? The services of a good lawyer who specializes in the transfer of businesses will be crucial in this event, but there are a few guidelines that may be stated here.

Healthy local newspapers, even very small ones, are widely seen as solid, attractive investments, and they usually sell for large sums. That might be one reason for starting your own paper and building it up into a valuable property. It also means that, unless you are willing to buy a paper that is in trouble, you may have to spend a huge amount to buy into this business. The opportunities for small, independent publishers to purchase newspapers are less now than in the past, partly because multi-million-dollar newspaper groups are buying up many of the available papers at astronomical prices.

How does one arrive at a fair price? There are a few generally accepted rules of thumb. One is that the value of a paper is roughly equal to its gross income for one year. Another method is to multiply the annual net income by ten. But there are many factors that might shift these estimates either higher or lower, most of them having to do with the vitality of the newspaper and its community. What is the size and character of the community? Is it in a state of growth or decline? What is the newspaper's paid circulation, and what percentage of its potential market actually subscribes? Are the accounts receivable in good shape, or does the newspaper have trouble collecting unpaid advertising bills? Does the geographical location of the paper make it more or less attractive in any way? When you buy a newspaper you are often buying little more than its typesetting equipment and the good will of its subscribers and advertisers—if either of these seems shaky, you might be better off starting a new publication in the same town rather than dragging around someone else's problems and reputation.

Starting from scratch: How much will it cost? If you are starting out on your own, your first question will probably be how much cash you must beg, borrow, or take out of the bank in order to get your newspaper going. The answer to this question depends largely on several factors: whether you are fully committed to the newspaper, or if you are merely testing the waters without a firm commitment to go on for a number of years; how willing you are to expend your own energy rather than spending money on time-saving equipment; and how much you can hope to collect in advertising revenues from the very first issue on.

Assuming you are not planning to pay out very much in salaries, the main thing you will need to spend money on before you start is the machinery you'll need to prepare camera-ready copy for the printer—typesetting equipment, that is, and a photostat camera if you want one. A discussion of how to approach the typesetting market appears in *Typography,* pages 54–64; but you might want to apply these guidelines to your decision:

¶ If your commitment to the newspaper is tentative, and you want to see how it is received before you put a lot of money into it, you are best off renting or leasing a typesetting system. Do not invest in a photostat camera; you can either get your stats from a graphic studio or print shop, or ask your printer to prepare whatever line and halftone work you need done.

¶ If you are determined to stick with the newspaper but you have no money at all to invest, take the same course: rent equipment, and have your printer take care of your line art and halftone work. Or take out a bank loan and buy an inexpensive used typesetting system for $5,000 to $10,000. Save the photostat camera for a more prosperous era; you can do without it. Either of these two courses should mean that you will be able to make your monthly payments with the money you take in from advertising and subscriptions.

¶ If you have $20,000 or more to invest at the start, buy a better, newer typesetter (such as a used EditWriter), along with a microcomputer and a printer to take care of your bookkeeping, and a photostat camera and processor. This will set you up in style.

Besides your investment in typesetting equipment, printing is the largest inescapable expense you will incur as you start up your paper. Printing costs will be determined by a number of variables (see page 42) and may differ considerably from one part of the country to another, but in our area, in 1983, you might reasonably expect to get 1,500 to 2,000 copies of a 16-page compact-size paper printed for $400. Calculate the projected size of your paper and estimate your printing costs on a per-issue basis, as you have already done with your typesetting costs.

The one other item that can significantly add to your per-issue cost is distribution. If you are starting a newspaper, the initial circulation drive will be expensive, because it can cost $100 or more to send out each thousand copies of a free mailing. You will also have to continue to pay third-class postage rates on your regular mailings until a second-class permit is approved. (See *Circulation and Distribution.*) Even though you can eventually recover the difference in cost between third- and second-class rates, the total amount you will have to put up before the permit is approved is likely to be large.

After the paper is established, other costs will take on greater significance. Chief among these will be the wages you pay your staff and yourself; the staff may be willing and able to work for nothing until business picks up, but if the paper is to have vitality, real remuneration, even in small amounts, is a necessity. Certainly by the end of the first year of publication all staff members and contributors should be paid.

The yearly business cycle. Although the costs of running a newspaper remain relatively constant throughout the year, the income from advertising does not. The Christmas season is invariably the best for selling ads, while in January and February "newspaper publishers eat snow," as our printer used to say. Things always improve in the spring, and the summer months are usually slower. The location of your paper can alter these general rules, however. If you're in a summer resort area, the hot months will be best for business. (Some weekly papers in resorts switch to twice-weekly publication during the summer.) Similarly, the winter will be a good season if you're publishing in a ski resort area. Business is usually better in election years, because of the political advertising.

It's important to take these seasonal variations into account when you're planning a budget for yourself. If you're starting a newspaper, for example, you might well plan to commence publication in September to take advantage of the fall peak in the business cycle. If you do that, though, don't make any false predictions of imminent wealth on December 31; wait until you've lived through the long, hard winter.

How many pages? Your printing, typesetting, labor, and mailing costs will depend to a large degree on the number of pages you produce in an average issue—which in turn depends principally on the amount of advertising you sell. The decision on how many pages to produce is both a financial and an aesthetic one; it will affect the way your newspaper comes across to its readers, and it will determine in some sense your chances for survival.

If you add up the number of column inches of advertising in an issue and divide it by the total number of column inches in the paper, the result is the percentage of advertising in that issue. For example, assume that you have chosen a four-column format and that the type page is 15 inches deep. Your paper thus has 60 (4 × 15) column inches per page. An eight-page issue would contain a total of 480 column inches, a twelve-page issue would contain 720 column inches, and a sixteen-page issue would have 960. Let's say you have sold 330 inches of advertising for a certain issue. If you publish only eight pages, the advertising portion will be 69 percent (330 ÷ 480). With a twelve-page issue, the same amount of advertising will constitute 46 percent (330 ÷ 720). In a sixteen-page issue, the advertising portion drops to 34 percent (330 ÷ 960).

We believe that the ideal proportion of ads in a small-format newspaper is between 40 and 50 percent. Of course, the decision on how many pages to print must also take into account the amount of news and other material that you have on hand. We often find ourselves choosing to run four extra pages just so we can get a long feature article or a set of especially good photographs into the paper. It costs more money to do things this way, but the reward is an attractive newspaper and satisfied, appreciative readers.

One way to keep the percentage of ads down without affecting profit is to raise your ad rates. The advertisers will tend to take smaller ads, but will probably end up spending the same amount of money—the only difference is that their ads will occupy less space, leaving more for the news. For example, let's say you charge $3 per column inch and you sell $1,500 worth of ads for an issue. That corresponds to 500 inches of advertising—or 52 percent in a sixteen-page paper containing 960 column inches. But if you raise the rate to $3.50, and you still sell $1,500 worth of ads, they will take up only 429 inches—or 45 percent of a sixteen-page issue. That can mean the difference between a crowded edition and a well-balanced one. At the same time, you should be careful not to set your ad rate so far above those of competing publications that you cause unnecessary difficulties for the salesperson.

Preparing a business plan. The next step in your preliminary financial planning is to prepare a business plan that sets forth your projected costs and income over a number of years. If you eventually decide to seek a loan from a bank, or to involve others in your business as limited partners or in some other fashion, a careful business plan will also stand you in good stead. And if you come to the point of deciding to sell your newspaper, it reflects well on you to have a methodical outline of your goals. The business plan should cover these matters:

1. *Description of the newspaper.* State the planned format, frequency of publication, and the basis of circulation (subscription, newsstand, free distribution, and so on).

2. *Description of the market area.* Is this a local newspaper or does it serve a regional or national interest group? The geographical area you plan to cover is important as an index of your potential advertising field.

3. *Your target readership.* How many potential readers do you have? (Be sure to include not only population figures but the number of households, which more accurately reflects the number of subscriptions you can generate.) What are their characteristics in terms of age, social or economic status, median income? Most particularly, where do they shop and what do they buy? Such information, again, directly affects your potential advertising income.

4. *The competition.* Are there other newspapers that serve the same readership? Describe and evaluate them, especially in terms of their circulation, frequency, format, advertising rates and revenues, strengths, and weaknesses. Analyze here the reasons you believe that another newspaper is viable.

5. *Projected income.* What will your advertising rates be? Estimate an advertising total for an average issue, and calculate overall advertising income for the next several years. (You can assume that these totals will fluctuate seasonally, and you should plan for them to gradually increase as your paper becomes established. Don't forget to figure in an annual hike of your ad rates.) Set a subscription rate, projecting appropriate increases in this as well; and estimate how many subscribers you will have for each of the coming few years. Estimate income from newsstand sales, and from any other possible sources of revenue.

6. *Projected expenses.* Carefully outline all possible expenses, estimated on a monthly or a per-issue basis. Are you paying off a loan from having bought the newspaper from someone else? Will you need to rent space and pay utility costs? What equipment will you require, and how will you pay for it? (This includes not only bigger items like a typesetting machine, a camera, or a small computer, but also office furniture, layout tables, and other less obvious items.) What services will you have need of—phone, attorney, accountant, insurance? What materials will you have to buy on a regular basis throughout the year—film and chemicals, photographic paper, printed bills and other paper products, and so forth? Project the staff you will need to hire, and their compensation (don't forget to include commissions on ad sales); and project allocations for outside contributors of editorial copy. Estimate your printing costs, based upon the

average size issue you plan to produce. And calculate how much it will cost you to distribute the newspaper, through the mail, home delivery, or other methods. Don't forget the costs of promotion.

7. *Your marketing plan.* How do you plan to introduce and promote your newspaper? Will you mail it to your entire target readership for the first several issues, or conduct a telephone subscription drive, or plan periodic special promotions involving local groups? Will you offer special rates to entice new readers? Eventually, of course, your paper will sell itself on the basis of its quality, but at the start few will have even heard of it, and you will need an imaginative marketing plan.

Types of business organization. There are several ways to organize a business, each with its own advantages and disadvantages. A *sole proprietorship* is in most respects the simplest. An individual or a married couple organized as a sole proprietorship can for all practical purposes go into business without doing much more than maintaining good records and filing information concerning their business on their individual tax returns.

Partnerships generally provide more flexibility in the operation, ownership, and financing of a business. Unless you are incorporated, some sort of legal partnership agreement must be developed if you intend to go into business with someone not your spouse. For tax purposes, each partner's share of the company's annual profits or losses is reported on his individual tax return.

One variety of partnership sometimes used to attract investors provides for two types of partners: *general* and *limited.* The general partners are responsible for the operation of the business, and may be legally liable if, for instance, a suit is brought against the company. The limited partners usually act as investors only. Their percentage of the company's profits or losses will be reported on their individual tax returns, and they would be able to realize capital gains if the business were eventually sold for profit, but their overall liability, financially and legally, is usually limited to the amount of their original investment.

A *corporation,* legally speaking, is the most complex and expensive sort of business organization to enter into. One reason that people choose to incorporate is that the corporate form is usually thought to provide the owners protection from certain legal and financial liabilities. But a corporation must file extensive and costly tax returns and other paperwork with state and federal agencies on a regular basis. One corporate form worth investigating, though, is the so-called *Subchapter S* corporation, which provides that, like a partnership, the company can pass its profits or losses on to the individual stockholders. This provision can make it possible to avoid the often higher tax rates that a corporation must pay on its profits. In any event, you should consult an accountant and a lawyer for more specific advice on business organization. If you represent a charitable, educational, scientific, or religious organization and intend to publish a newspaper on a nonprofit basis, get expert advice on the legal requirements for such an operation.

A good book including some concise and helpful discussion of the pros and cons of proprietorships, partnerships, and corporations is *Honest Business* by Michael Phillips and Salli Rasberry, published by Random House.

SETTING UP A BOOKKEEPING SYSTEM

Talk to your accountant about the best ways to set up your business books and records and about the requirements of state and federal tax laws. If you are so inclined, there is no reason why you can't handle your own book-keeping work without the assistance of an accountant. Many small businesses are acquiring microcomputers to streamline their operations, and of course such computers are capable of many wonders. We found, though, upon looking into software packages available for small computers, that there was nothing that could efficiently and easily fulfill the specific and often peculiar bookkeeping functions of a small newspaper— keeping advertising records, sending bills, and paying commissions; maintaining subscription files; and paying staff and contributors. To meet our computer needs adequately we were compelled to have a new software package written especially for small newspapers; we are happy to supply it to others in the newspaper business, for a fee comparable to other software packages. (For more information, write to us at P.O. Box 308, Harvard, Massachusetts 01451.)

It is also perfectly possible to do all your bookkeeping without a computer, as we did for our first ten years of operation. The basic components of the system—and the ones on which our computer system is founded—are as follows:

¶ *A filing system* for the classification of incoming mail. Get yourself a date stamp and mark each piece of mail with the date of its receipt. All payments of any sort should go into one box; other boxes can be set up for press releases, classified ads, bills, changes of address, and so on.

¶ *A general ledger,* or cash account book. This is simply a big book in which you will enter every single financial transaction related to the newspaper. In one section you will note each payment you receive, along with the date, who paid it, what it was for, and whether it was by cash or check. In another section you will enter each business-related disbursement that you make, together with the date, the name of the payee, the reason for the payment, and so on. By adding up the amounts in the receipts section you arrive at the newspaper's gross income. Adding up the disbursements (and making any necessary adjustments, such as for depreciation) gives you the total expenses. By subtracting this figure from gross income you arrive at your net income, or, if the expenses total is the larger, the net loss.

¶ *An advertising account book*. This can be a large three-ring binder; it will contain the account records of every significant advertiser and will be used for sending out bills and statements and for recording ad payments. (See section on billing and collection below.)

¶ *Subscription files* containing a record card for each subscriber. They are discussed in detail in the preceding chapter.

¶ *A payroll book*. This will contain a separate page for each of your regular employees. Because most of the people who work for you will be paid on a free-lance basis, you will need to record each item of service that they render—each news story, photograph, or drawing; each hour of typesetting or pasteup work; each ad commission.

¶ *A circulation record book*. This will contain a running total of your circulation figures from issue to issue, newsstand sales records, and the like. It is fully described in the preceding chapter.

¶ *An advertising checklist file,* containing lists of the ads in your newspaper arranged by issue date and by salesperson (see *Advertising,* pages 113–114). It will be used, among other purposes, to keep tabs on delinquent advertising accounts.

Designing your own forms. The various parts of your bookkeeping system will require different books and forms on which you can record information in a neat and organized fashion. Some of these can be purchased at any good business supply store. Others can be ordered from mail-order companies that deal in individualized business forms. But it is quite easy to design your own forms, set the type for them and lay them out yourself, and then have them printed up inexpensively at a nearby quick-printing shop.

The subscription record cards, renewal notices, and gift announcements shown in the preceding chapter are good examples. You should also have your own invoice-statements, advertising acount sheets, advertising rate sheets, and weekly ad checklists.

Bank accounts and record-keeping. Because you will be processing a large number of checks, it is important to have an efficient way of handling them. In particular, avoid any mingling of newspaper finances with your personal finances. You should have a separate business checking account into which you deposit all business income and from which you write checks to cover all business expenses. (There may be some exceptions: if, for example, your business office is also your home, a portion of your rent, electricity, heating, and telephone costs will count as legitimate business expenses. But unless you want to write two checks to pay each bill—one for the business part and one for the nonbusiness part—you will probably use your personal checks for these things, entering only the proper portion of each payment in your disbursement ledger. See additional comments below on using your home as an office.)

Because most of your business expenses will be paid by check, the entries in your checkbook will to a great extent duplicate those in the disbursement section of your general ledger. Though this may seem to be unnecessary bookkeeping work, it is a very good idea to keep such detailed records as a way of checking yourself when you find an error or in the event that some of your books are lost or destroyed.

One of the main reasons for keeping scrupulously accurate records is for income tax purposes. If your tax return is audited, you will need to produce evidence to substantiate all of the payments that you have claimed as business expenses. You should get a receipt for any item paid for with cash, and duly file it away where you can find it again easily. Another reason why your books should be in good order is that the postal inspectors may call on you unexpectedly and demand proof that the subscribers' copies mailed under your second-class permit have actually been paid for. In order to provide such proof, you should have entered on each subscriber's record card the date and amount of his payment; from there you should be able to go to the appropriate date in your general ledger and find an entry noting the subscriber's name, the amount of his payment, and the bank number of his check; from there you should be able to go to the file in which you have carefully saved all of your bank deposit slips and find the one that included that particular subscriber's check. (If the subscription was paid in cash, that fact should be noted in the ledger and a copy of the subscriber's receipt kept in a file.) In order to accomplish this, of course, you must have written in your ledger the bank number of each subscription check, and you must also have filled out your deposit slips correctly, again noting the bank number of each check.

Aside from the pressures that agents of the government can exert on you, there are other excellent reasons for maintaining orderly books. If you have been doing the work yourself and one day you decide to turn the job over to a bookkeeper, or if your bookkeeper suddenly quits and you have to break in a new one, the ease of the transition will be directly related to the orderliness of your system. Also, if the day comes when you decide to sell your newspaper, a good bookkeeping system will be one of the basic prerequisites of the sale.

The single most important factor in successful bookkeeping is your willingness to take the time to do it properly. Each entry must be legible and self-explanatory to someone (other than the person who wrote it) looking at it years later. If there are special circumstances surrounding a particular item that would cause it to appear wrong or confusing later on, explain it fully in the books. Don't assume that you'll remember the details—you won't. Bookkeeping work, like weeding a garden, must be done regularly and religiously; if you let it go for too long it becomes an almost overwhelming task to rcover the lost ground. If you find the work distasteful or you simply don't have the time, hire a bookkeeper. The investment will be more than worthwhile.

Shop around at different banks before choosing the one at which to open your business account. A commercial bank will not necessarily offer the best choice. In New England, for example, savings banks are allowed to offer their customers interest-bearing checking accounts (so-called NOW accounts); some banks also provide checking accounts that are free of service charges under certain conditions. This can save you a lot of money, compared with a commercial bank account in which you must pay a service charge for every check and every item deposited. Be sure you know exactly what kinds of service charges you will have to pay before you open an account.

Have a rubber stamp made up to read "For deposit only to the account of _____" and including your bank account number. This will save a great deal of time in endorsing checks.

BILLING AND COLLECTIONS

Most of your newspaper's income will consist of payments from advertisers, and so it is of the greatest importance that advertising bills be sent out promptly and that careful records be kept of your accounts. You should have a large advertising account book containing a page for each advertiser.

Advertising account sheet.

We have sheets specially designed for this purpose printed up on stiff index stock (see example); our computer program, too, is designed on this model, with a file for each advertiser. We send out bills to advertisers once a month. You may find it worthwhile in some cases to bill more promptly; for example, if you have a one-time large ad near the beginning of the month you might not want to wait until the end of the month to send the bill. Under no circumstances should your billings be less frequent than once a month.

The billing process. When it's time to sit down and do the monthly bills start by assembling a copy of each issue of the newspaper published during the month. Going through the papers page by page, you then make an informal list of advertisers, in alphabetical order, including the date, size, and price of each ad. Cross off the ad in the newspaper as you enter it on this list. This informal list can be double-checked against the weekly advertising check-lists submitted by your ad salesperson and filled out for any uncommissioned ads as well. (Any ads that have been paid for in advance should be so marked on the weekly checklists—that way you will know not to send bills for them.)

When the informal alphabetical list is completed, go through the advertising book page by page and make out a bill for every advertiser on your list for that month. In addition, make out a statement for each advertiser with an outstanding balance from previous months, even though he has not done any advertising in the current billing period. (The difference between a "bill"—or "invoice"—and a "statement" is that the former describes and calls for payment for one or more specific items that have not been previously billed, while the latter is a complete statement of account for all unpaid items including those previously billed.) Be sure to enter all of the appropriate information on the advertiser's account sheet at the same time that you make out his statement. You will need some kind of invoice-statement form, of course; these may be ordered pre-printed, or you can design your own (see example).

If you have a complicated system of advertising rates and discounts, you will have to indicate the appropriate rate for each ad on the bill and on the advertiser's account sheet. (See the discussion of rates and discounts in *Advertising,* page 101.) We prefer to keep our bookkeeping simple by having just one rate for commercial advertising and by giving volume discounts only when the advertiser's bill exceeds a certain amount in any one month. Our experience has been that more complicated discount systems, including those based on frequency of advertising, often lead to problems and disputes. For example, you might agree to give a merchant a 15 percent

The Harvard Post

Harvard, Mass. 01451

—STATEMENT—

To: _____   Date: _____

_____

_____

_____

                                                    Amount

For: _____ $_____

_____   _____

_____   _____

_____   _____

_____   _____

                    Sub-Total: $_____

Discount (if any): _____%   —_____

                    Sub-Total: $_____

            Previous Balance: _____

Please pay this amount   TOTAL: $_____

Comments:

An all-purpose bill and statement form.

discount for running an ad every week for the next year. After four months, though, the merchant decides to cancel his advertising. You are within your rights in this situation to bill the advertiser retroactively for his four months of discounts, but actually collecting that money may well turn out to be a problem.

Every advertiser should have the opportunity to make sure that his ad actually appeared in the newspaper and was free from errors. We send a complete copy of each issue to every advertiser represented therein, addressing them and mailing them at the same time that we send out subscribers' copies. Other newspapers simply send tear sheets of the ads along with the bills. Some advertisers may request tear sheets in addition to receiving a complete copy of the issue. Others may require duplicate copies of bills so that they can be reimbursed for *co-op ads,* that is, ads that are partly paid for by someone else—usually a large corporation that subsidizes local advertising of its products. All such special requirements should be noted on the advertising account sheet. Make sure that your ad rep relays to the bookkeeper any special requests from advertisers by means of marginal remarks on the weekly checklist.

Advertisers with overdue balances from previous bills should be gently reminded that you would appreciate their prompt payment. The newspaper advertising bill is, unfortunately, often one of the last ones to be paid, especially by the struggling merchant who is skeptical of the value of his ads to begin with. Therefore, you must carefully monitor your advertising accounts for possible trouble. More is said on this subject below. Very often, though, all that is needed to produce a payment is a friendly handwritten comment at the bottom of the statement.

When all the bills for the month have been made out and all the envelopes addressed, check through the entire pile one more time before sealing and mailing them. Make sure that the numbers add up correctly, that the names and dates are right, that the proper discounts have been applied, and so on.

Errors and disputes. Many newspapers print a disclaimer near the front of each issue saying that the paper will not be responsible for losses caused by typographical errors in advertisements but will reprint that part of the ad in which the error occurred. In some cases, of course, giving the advertiser free space in the next issue will not make up for the error; for example, if the date of a special one-time sale was misprinted, a correction the next week, after the event, will not help at all. The only reasonable policy is to offer the victim of an error the choice of a partial discount on either the ad that has already run or a subsequent one. The size of the discount should be commensurate with the seriousness of the error; misspelling the name of an advertised item, for instance, is not as bad as getting the price wrong. But it's usually a good idea to be generous in such situations. You will be much better off in the long run impressing the aggrieved advertiser with your sympathy and magnanimity than with your stinginess—he will be more inclined to give you another try.

On the other hand, you will occasionally come across a nasty character who habitually complains about insignificant or imagined defects in his ads; asserts that he wanted that ad to run only twice, not three times; won't pay his bills on time; and generally gives your ad salesperson a hard time. Give this type of advertiser only so much rope, and then cut him loose.

Collecting overdue bills. This is probably the single most unpleasant part of the newspaper business; it is also one that can take up a large part of your time and energy if you let it. The best way to avoid all this irritation is by means of careful bookkeeping and an astute advertising representative. Don't let overdue accounts go from month to month without attention. Don't automatically extend credit to unfamiliar or new businesses. Don't let your representative sell ads to those with unreasonably overdue bills. And don't do business at all with people who have burned you before, except on a strictly cash-in-advance basis.

An easy way to keep track of overdue advertising accounts is by means of the weekly ad checklists. Our lists have a column on the far right labeled "Paid"; when a payment is received from an advertiser, the appropriate ads are checked off on the various lists. Thus, by looking through our chronological file of weekly checklists we can quickly spot those advertisers who are due for a little encouragement.

It is important to send monthly statements to every outstanding account. These alone will bring in a fair number of payments. A simple handwritten note at the bottom of the statement will often help. After whatever you consider an unreasonable amount of time has elapsed (two months, three months, four months—it all depends on the size of the bill, your patience, and the persistence of your own creditors) call the delinquent advertiser on the telephone and ask if there is any problem with your bill, and, if not, whether you can expect payment within a specific number of days. When those days have passed and you still haven't gotten any money it's time for another telephone call or, better yet, a personal visit.

Obviously, this routine can go on forever with some people. At some point you will have to decide (1) to turn the account over to a collection agency (which will take a substantial percentage of any money collected); (2) to file suit in a small-claims or other court; or (3) to give up. Filing in small-claims court is a simple procedure and can be accomplished without a lawyer in many states; there is usually a fairly low limit on the amount of money that may be involved. Find out how to do it by asking the clerk of a local court, your town clerk, state representative, consumer protection agency, or a friendly lawyer. A favorable judgment in small-claims court, however, does not necessarily mean that you will ever collect your money. Winning the judgment is one thing; enforcing it is something else.

After a while you will begin to develop a sixth sense about slow-paying advertisers. You will learn which ones are basically honest, though disorganized, and which ones keep putting you off again and again with false promises. Some people seem never to look at the bills that come in the mail, but will pay you cheerfully when you present the bill in person. As you grow more sensitive to these subtleties the number of losses you incur will decrease. In general, personal attention and concern will prove to be the most persuasive force in your bill-collection arsenal. Try to remember that others besides you have financial problems, even though none of them is so foolhardy as to try to make a living by newspapering.

Classified ads. As we have already said, we don't think it worth the trouble to send out bills for classifieds. The amount of money involved is usually small compared to the accompanying bookkeeping. If you do set up a classified billing system, a simple card file is probably the best choice. Send out the bill for each ad immediately instead of waiting till the end of the month, and encourage advertisers to pay in advance by offering a substantial discount. In fact, there is nothing wrong with insisting on advance payment for all classified advertising.

Subscription bills. The handling of subscription records is discussed in detail in Chapter 9. Besides your regular renewal notices, you will have to send out bills for subscriptions that are not prepaid. This task should be done at frequent intervals, preferably as soon after the subscription starts as possible. Note the date of billing on the subscriber's record card, and send a reminder (or make a telephone call) if a month or so goes by without your receiving the payment.

Computerized billing. The program we have designed to handle our accounts is modeled after the system we have just described. Each advertiser has a file in the computer, with the dates and sizes of each ad recorded, along with the dates and amounts of bills and payments. When an advertiser agrees to take an ad, this information is entered in his file. Ad rates and discount information have already been entered in the computer's memory, so calculations of how much the advertiser owes are automatic. At any time, you can ask the computer to search for all advertisers who have agreed to advertise on a certain date, which allows you to make up ad checklists each week at deadline time.

At your regular billing time, you ask the computer to call up the names of all advertisers with unpaid accounts, both from the billing period just past and from all previous billing periods. The computer will then generate bills for the entire list, along with mailing labels if you so desire. If you want a list of all outstanding accounts over two months old, or all advertisers who owe more than a certain amount, so you can bill them early, it is simple and quick to search them out.

Subscription files are also entered in the computer, which can generate mailing lists for renewal notices as well as bills at a moment's notice.

THE PAYROLL

You will have to worry about setting up a payroll system only if you decide to pay people. During the first months of publication at the Harvard Post we didn't pay anyone except the printer. It is possible to run a small newspaper on this basis because there are usually a few people in any community who are willing to write or make other contributions for nothing, or next to nothing. They may do this out of a desire for journalistic experience, or a sense of community involvement, or simply for the ego-thrilling sensation of seeing one's own byline in the newspaper.

There is nevertheless a related sensation, perhaps equally thrilling, that comes from receiving a check in the mail in payment for one's journalistic efforts. We think it is a good idea to start paying your contributors as soon as it is economically possible, even if the amounts of money are insignificant. Even after your newspaper is on its feet and showing a profit, you will probably not be able to compensate your contributors to the extent that they really deserve. You will therefore have a continuing dependence on people who work for you more out of love than a desire for money. These contributors will be among your most valuable assets—treat them well.

The advertising representative is another matter. Hers is probably the most difficult job of all, as well as one of the most essential, and there are no bylines to make up for a skimpy paycheck. Furthermore, good advertising salespeople are hard to find, and if you are lucky enough to have one by all means pay her or him a reasonably attractive amount, and do anything else you can to keep that person on your staff.

How much to pay? It will be of interest to you to find out how much other newspapers in your area pay their employees and contributors. Almost all small papers pay their writers, photographers, and artists on a free-lance basis, and the fees paid are usually quite low. Set up a system for yourself that is easy to work with; you might pay a flat fee of five or ten dollars, for example, for every article, picture, or drawing. Another way to handle written contributions is to pay by the inch. Reporters who cover meetings of town committees for the Harvard Post are paid a basic fee of $7.50 for going to the meeting, plus 40 cents for each inch of copy that is used in the newspaper. (The pay-by-the-inch plan sometimes leads reporters to pad their stories with wordy constructions and unnecessary details; a strict editorial eye is needed here.)

Many newspapers pay their advertising salespeople a basic weekly salary, in return for which the ad rep is expected to fulfill a quota. For example, the salesperson might be paid $150 a week and be expected to come up with $750 worth of ads. If the quota is exceeded, an additional commission of 6, 8, or 10 percent on the extra sales is paid to the ad rep as a bonus. If the salesperson doesn't meet the quota occasionally, nothing happens. But if the quota goes unmet regularly, then either a new ad rep is found or the publisher is somehow persuaded that the quota has been set at an unreasonably high level.

The quota system has its problems for the very small newspaper operation. The advertising sales total is likely to fluctuate widely, especially at the beginning, and making a commitment to pay a weekly salary when the size of a reasonable quota is difficult to judge can result in money trouble for the publisher. It is probably wiser under these circumstances to pay the advertising representative only a small weekly stipend designed to cover basic expenses, and for the rest of the salesperson's remuneration to be paid on a straight commission basis. The amount of the commission should certainly not be less than 15 percent. An approximate quota should be established anyway, based on the amount of money that you have calculated to be necessary for the operation of your paper. (See additional remarks below on paying the advertising representative.)

Other people on your staff, such as bookkeepers, typographers, layout artists, circulation people, and other helpers, can be paid on an hourly basis, also as free-lancers. It is best to have as few salaried employees as possible (assuming that you can afford to have any at all), because of the requirements for payroll deductions for such workers. If you have an office outside your home, you will probably have to hire someone to be in it and answer the telephone more or less full-time. This person can easily double as bookkeeper or typographer, or any number of other things. (For instance, the person in the office must be able to sell advertisng space to businesspeople who come in off the street wanting to advertise.) But most of your staff members will work only part-time, and should be paid a specific amount for each item of work they produce or for each hour spent on the job. In order to keep track of all these items you need a payroll book.

The payroll book. This is simply a looseleaf binder containing a page for every one of your employees. Each item for which the employee is to be paid should be entered on a separate line on the appropriate page; the entry should include the date, a brief explanation of the item, and the amount of money.

As soon after the publication of each issue of your paper as you can, go through the issue marking every story, column, photograph, and drawing that must be paid for. Make the proper entry in your payroll book for each item. Entries for employees who work on an hourly basis should be made each day that they work; be sure that you and the employee agree on the exact amount of time that is to be paid for. Or you can have the hourly employees submit work slips each day or week showing the number of hours worked. At the end of the month (or other agreed-upon period) go through the payroll book, add up the amounts to be paid on each employee's page, and write checks, entering the dates and amounts of the payments in the book. Each person should receive with his or her check a clear listing of the items that it covers.

Each month you should figure out exactly how much money is going out to the staff, and you should compare these figures with your total income for the same period. This will allow you to judge whether you are being too generous or too stingy, besides giving you a good indication of the financial progress of your enterprise.

Paying the advertising representative. If you pay your salesperson by commission you will face a special bookkeeping problem. First, you have to decide when the ad rep gets paid for the ads that have been sold—at the end of the month in which they appeared in the paper, or not until the ads in question have actually been paid for by the advertisers? If your cash reserves are low you may want to choose the latter system. It also serves as an encouragement to the salesperson to stay away from merchants who are unlikely to pay for their ads. You can decide for yourself whether you think it is fair for the ad rep to have to share some of the loss in the case of an uncollectable bill. We think it is fair. It is also possible to employ a combination of the two systems: pay the salesperson half the commission right away, then the other half when the ad is paid for; or pay her an advance against commissions (tantamount to a salary) which is then deducted from future commission payments. Because the advertising representative is such an important part of your organization, your method of compensating her should be flexible; you should be willing to tailor it somewhat to her particular financial needs.

If the arrangement you choose depends in some way on payments for ads actually having been received, you must set up special payroll sheets for the advertising representative. These should be kept in the payroll book. Every time an ad payment comes in from one of the salesperson's accounts, the date and amount of the payment and the name of the advertiser should be entered on the sheet. At the end of the month all the payments for that period are added up and the total commission is calculated. Along with the paycheck, the salesperson should also receive a detailed listing of the advertisers from whom payments were received that month. You should also provide her with a list of those whose accounts are overdue, along with your comments on who you think is a safe bet and who ought to be approached with caution.

Our computer accounting program makes this procedure much simpler. When an ad payment is received, the computer automatically calculates the commission and records it in the appropriate salesperson's account. At any time, as frequently as you desire, you can call up a complete list of ad commissions and pay your representative.

If your ad rep doesn't get her commission until the ads are paid for, she will probably want to try collecting the money herself. If she is willing to act as your agent in this way, encourage her; but stipulate that all such payments be made by check and not cash.

The salesperson's weekly ad checklist is the key to several aspects of your business and production work. It is this list that shows who sold a particular ad for a particular week; this is especially important if you have more than one person selling for you, or when you are making the transition from a retiring ad rep to a new one. The list also serves as a double check on the proper size and price for each ad. It is used in layout to make sure that each ad sold is really in place in the newspaper before it goes off to the printer. It provides a quick way to determine the total amount of space needed for advertising in a particular issue, as well as the total advertising income for that week. And finally, the checklist file serves as a simple means to keep track of advertisers who are late in paying you.

It is important, then, for the weekly ad checklist to be filled out neatly and accurately. Make sure your advertising representative knows what you expect from her or him in this connection.

A SUMMARY OF BOOKKEEPING

Though newspaper bookkeeping practices vary according to the size and frequency of publication and the complexity of the bookkeeping system, the following general guidelines should be helpful:

Every day you should process all incoming checks and other payments and prepare your bank deposit. Make sure that the bookkeeper knows and follows the correct procedure for posting each type of payment in the records. Subscribers' payments should be entered on the subscription record cards and in the general ledger. Payments from advertisers should be entered on the advertisers' account sheets and the ledger, and checked off on the weekly advertising checklists. In addition, if your ad rep is paid by commission, the advertisers' payments should be entered on the salesperson's payroll record.

Every week the subscription files should be brought up to date by entering new subscribers, making any address changes, and removing those that have been canceled. Bills should be sent out to new subscribers who have not paid in advance. As soon as each edition of the paper is published those who have contributed to it should have their contributions entered on their payroll sheets. Some newspapers also send bills to their advertisers every week, as soon as the ads appear.

Every month bills should be sent to advertisers (unless this is done more frequently). Subscription renewal notices and reminders should be sent to the appropriate subscribers. The payroll figures for the month should be added up and checks sent to all employees and contributors. The ad rep should also receive an up-to-date listing of the advertisers whose accounts are past due, together with the publishers' comments on specific cases. In addition, it is a good idea to add up your various expenses and receipts every month or so and thus arrive at totals for advertising income, subscription income, newsstand sales, gross income, payroll expenses, utilities and general expenses, net income, and circulation. Keeping track of these figures will enable you to gauge your progress and to make projections for the future.

TAXES

Even if the very sight of IRS Form 1040 gives you a stomachache and you intend to let your accountant take care of the whole mess for you, it is nevertheless useful to understand how the tax laws work and to know exactly what is in your own tax return. You must think about your taxes well in advance of the annual April 15 deadline; as a self-employed person running a small business you will have special obligations that must be discharged at the proper times and on the proper pieces of paper. At the same time, the tax laws favor businesses in many ways and you should take advantage of this wherever possible. If you don't have an accountant you will undoubtedly need tax advice at some point; get hold of all the forms and instruction pamphlets well ahead of time and go through them making a list of questions to ask of an expert. You are probably better off paying an accountant or tax lawyer for a consultation than trying to get accurate answers directly from the Internal Revenue Service. The IRS can be very hard to get on the telephone and, in our experience, the information that you do get is as likely as not to be wrong. The IRS does publish some useful guides, and a good way to begin your taxation education is by asking the nearest tax forms distribution center to send you Publication Number 334, "Tax Guide for Small Business," and Publication Number 552, "Record-keeping Requirements and a Guide to Tax Publications." Another good item to have around is Form 4868, "Application for Automatic Extension of Time to File U.S. Individual Income Tax Return."

Record-keeping. The single most important technique for avoiding apoplexy at tax time is to keep neat, accurate records all year long. Ideally, you should be able to total up the income and expense figures in your ledger at the end of the year and transfer them directly to the tax forms. If you break down your expenses into categories—salaries, rent, printing, postage, office supplies, and so on—as you go along, you will have that much less work to do at year's end. Set up a good filing system and be sure to save all your canceled checks, bank statements, deposit slips, and receipts. If you are using a computer, keep hard copies of all your records as well (you can generate them on your computer printer), and make copies of all diskettes in case the originals are destroyed.

Be sure to read the section on books and records in the IRS Tax Guide for Small Business, mentioned above. Another useful IRS publication is Number 583, "Recordkeeping for a Small Business."

Tax forms. The actual forms you use will depend somewhat on the organization of your business. If it is a sole proprietorship (owned entirely by you and your spouse) you will use Schedule C, "Profit or (Loss) from Business or Profession," in addition to Form 1040. If it is a partnership or joint venture you will use Form 1065, "U.S. Partnership Return of Income," and the individual partners will show their shares of the profit or loss on their own personal tax returns. If you have formed a corporation you will probably use Form 1120, "U.S. Corporation Income Tax Return." In some respects different rules apply to the three kinds of business organization; in the case of either a partnership or corporation, expert tax advice is essential.

You may need to request other forms and publications from the IRS. Self-employed people generally must report their income and pay social security taxes by using Schedule SE. You may also be required to make estimated tax payments; this is done on Form 1040–ES. Other situations that apply to you may call for Form 2441, "Credit for Child Care Expenses"; Form 3468, "Computation of Investment Credit"; Form 5329, "Return for Individual Retirement Savings Arrangement"; or any number of other forms. The Tax Guide for Small Business is a good place to find out about these things.

You are also required to report to the IRS your payments to employees. If you withhold taxes from these payments, you must obtain an Employer Identification Number and use Form W–2; if you do not make any withholding you will use Form 1099–MISC. (See additional remarks about employee taxes.)

The advantages of self-employment. We are not talking here about the psychological rewards of being the boss but about tax benefits that the small businessperson enjoys. Many expenses that the ordinary salaried employee must pay taxes on are legitimate business deductions for the self-employed person. For example, if the employee uses his family car to commute to work he may not deduct the expenses incurred from his taxable income. But a small-newspaper publisher who uses the family car to drive to town meetings so he can report on them, to take the layout sheets to the printer and pick up the finished newspapers, and then to deliver the papers to the post office and the newsstands, may count all of this driving as a business expense and deduct it at the going rate (currently twenty cents per mile for the first 15,000 miles, ten cents per mile thereafter). When the newspaper owner buys a new car, moreover, he may claim an investment tax credit and depreciate its cost over a period of years to the extent that it is used in his business.

Some of these tax benefits are large and some are small, but all are worth taking advantage of. If you go out to dinner, write a review of the place and deduct the cost of the meal. If you find that your subscription to the daily newspaper in a nearby city is useful in editing your own local news, deduct the cost as a business expense. These are legitimate deductions, even though you might have gone to the restaurant or subscribed to the daily paper anyway.

One of the most significant tax benefits available to the small-newspaper owner is the use of his home as an office, though the rules relating to this practice are somewhat stricter than now than in years past.

Using your home as an office. Depending on the size of your home and the availability and cost of commercial office space in your town, you may decide to conduct business from your residence. There are many advantages to doing so. Establishing a separate office is expensive—you must pay for rent, utilities, telephone service, and someone to sit there all day—and it is not really necessary in most cases. Most of your business can be conducted by mail or phone; you simply need space for layout tables, typesetting machine, a desk or two, and some files.

You may deduct as a business expense a portion of the cost of running your home that is proportional to the percentage of the space used for business purposes. If the house has ten rooms and four of them are devoted to your newspaper, then you may deduct 40 percent of the household costs —rent, heat, electricity, repairs, insurance, and so on. If three-fourths of the use of your telephone is related to business, then deduct 75 percent of the cost of your monthly service. The 1976 tightening of the tax rules regarding business use of the home boils down to this: the areas of the house that you claim to be "office" space must be used *exclusively* for that purpose. Just because you conducted a newspaper interview in your living room you are not justified in designating it as business space for tax purposes. For this reason, it is important to separate the office areas of your home from the family areas. For more detailed information on this subject, send for IRS Publication Number 587, "Business Use of Your Home."

There are, of course, a number of disadvantages to working in your home. If you do not live near the central business district, you will miss out on a certain amount of walk-in business. More important, you will find it hard to get away from your work when it becomes important to do so. People will call you at all hours with trivial questions, classified ads, and "hot tips." (You might want to install a separate business phone, expensive but unpluggable, to get around this.) And, ultimately, you may fnd that your home is simply too distracting an environment for you to get your work done. Nevertheless, for the fledgling newspaper with limited resources the home office offers a very economical alternative.

Employee taxes. One of the best reasons for paying your employees on a free-lance or commission basis is that you will thus avoid the need for withholding taxes from their paychecks. As long as the amounts that you are paying people are relatively small and come in irregular chunks, and the people do not work in your office under your direct supervision, you do not have to worry about withholding. Those who draw a regular salary or work regular hours in your office generally are subject to withholding. Consult an accountant to find out exactly what your obligations are as an employer.

At the end of the calendar year you should send to each of your employees a tax form showing the total amount paid to him during the year. For those on withholding this will be done on Form W–2; free-lance and commissioned workers should receive Form 1099–MISC. More information on this subject may be found in IRS Publication Number 539, "Withholding Taxes and Reporting Requirements."

THE FINAL ANALYSIS

To produce a small newspaper is to be engaged in several degrees of planning ahead—that is, making guesses about the future—ranging from
deciding how many pages to print in the next issue, to setting your advertising rates, to calculating the amount of money you can afford to pay your
staff, to making a long-term projection of the ultimate profitability of your
venture. If you have followed the procedures outlined earlier in this chapter,
you will have some good tools for making some educated guesses. Now you
will want to know the answer to the big question: Can you make it?

Let's say you have decided to start a newspaper. The gamble that you
are taking is whether the paper that you envision has a chance of succeeding
before you are driven to surrender by lack of money, lack of sleep, or loss of
sanity. Many factors must be considered: the size of the community of
readers you plan to serve, and their relative affluence; the size and the
vitality of the business community that serves this readership; the existence
of competing newspapers, and their quality; and, finally, your own abilities
and interests, as well as those of the people who will be working with you.
Talk to as many people in the community as you can to get an idea of how
they would receive a new newspaper, and to enlist their support. If there is
already a paper in the area, find out what its ad rates are and figure out what
its weekly ad income is. Its circulation figures will be revealing as well.

Most small-town weeklies have circulations equal to between 10
percent and 40 percent of the population of the area they serve. (We're
talking about paid circulation, of course.) A well-written newspaper that
covers local events thoroughly and objectively should have no trouble
reaching a circulation equal to 20 percent of the population within about
three years of its starting up. So if your community has 10,000 people in it,
and they are not already served by a good newspaper, you can reasonably
expect to build up a circulation of at least 2,000 within three years.

Make a list of all the businesses in and around your community that
might advertise in your paper. Try to figure out how much money they
spend on advertising, and how much of that you can reasonably attract
once your paper is established. With these figures you can estimate the
income that your newspaper will produce. Let's say you think you can get
an average of $800 worth of avertising per issue over the course of the year;
if you publish 50 issues, that comes to $40,000 of advertising annually. And
let's say your circulation goal is 2,000, and your subscription price will be
$10 per year; that comes to another $20,000. Your gross annual income goal
is thus $60,000.

Now you must estimate your production costs. Get bids from printers,
and figure out how you will set type. Decide which jobs you will do yourself,

and which ones you will hire others to do; then figure out how much you'll have to pay the others. Let's say you think you can hold your costs to an average of $1,000 per issue; that comes to $50,000 a year, and leaves $10,000 for you. Can you manage on that? For how long?

The first months and years are invariably hard ones for a new newspaper, and the amount of money that goes into this starting-up period will depend entirely on you. By concentrating on keeping expenses low and quality high, you can survive the lean years. And it is widely accepted that an established newspaper—especially a local one—is one of the solidest businesses you can own.

At just about the time that your paper is finally getting on its feet, you will probably find that some upstart has had the gall to decide to publish his own competing newspaper. This is not a cause for panic; on the contrary, it is a sure indication of your own success. As one of our favorite business advisers says, "Competition either exists or will develop." Moreover, competition in the newspaper business often turns out to be good for everyone. It is a sure incentive for publishers and editors to improve their papers, and it excites in the reading public an essential interest in local affairs and in the written word itself and the ways different writers with differing points of view can turn the same words to opposite purposes. There was a time when in hundreds of communities across this country citizens eagerly bought and read two or more different newspapers in order to follow the spirited journalistic rivalries that were played out in their pages. This book is written in the hope that such days may come again.

11 Deadlines

IT MAY WELL BE that of all the technical aspects of newspaper work, the function of deadlines is the most widely misunderstood. The deadline seems to the inexperienced to be a perfectly concrete thing: a dividing line in time and space, much like the moment when a subway train suddenly closes its doors. In fact, the newspaper deadline has virtually no substantive existence. It is rather like a photon; the energy of its approach can exert considerable influence on those it approaches, but if it is pinned down and examined it is found to be utterly weightless.

A deadline is completely useless once it has arrived. Its function is entirely psychological. Unfortunately, its effects vary widely from one person to the next, and this fact is the cause of much grief in editors. For example, there are a very few people—God bless them—who always beat a deadline with room to spare; they seem to be temperamentally incapable of allowing a deadline to approach too near. Much more common is the person who meets the deadline at precisely the last moment; this type likes to live dangerously and tempt fate. There is more to it than that, though. The deadline holds tremendous power over the last-moment person. It energizes him; its imminence is often the only thing that will enable him to accomplish the task at hand—whether it is writing an article or calling in a classified ad.

There is, of course, another category that is discouragingly large: those who cannot meet a deadline at all. There are many types within this group. Some are in fact quite dependable and will always show up with the required material, say, four hours late. They are closely related to the last-moment people; only for them the energizing power of the deadline is slightly delayed, and guilt begins to play an auxiliary role. Then there are others, for whom deadlines become a malignant presence long after they have passed. These people are generally not inspired by deadlines; first they ignore them, later they are depressed by them.

How does all this affect the way a newspaper should set up its deadlines? It depends in part on the editors' own deadline psychology. Keep in mind that very few of your correspondents will turn in their material ahead of time; so if you like to have room to spare you'd better set your deadlines well in advance. On the other hand, people soon learn what the "real" deadline is—especially the last-minute people. They hate artificial deadlines. Only the real thing for them.

Part of the problem is that the people on whom you depend for copy see their own deadline as the final curtain. They are too busy with their own agonized struggle to think about what you must go through between their deadline and yours. You can try to impress upon them the seriousness of the matter by describing in great detail the consequences of their tardiness: your frenzied last-minute editing, typesetting, cutting and pasting; your sleepless nights, violent outbursts of temper, disrupted family life.

But it won't do any good. Nothing does. We could tell you to set up a strict deadline schedule for each aspect of your newspaper production schedule—an early news deadline, a classified ad deadline, deadlines for feature stories, display ads, late news—arranging the whole operation so that you were finished each week on deadline day at five o'clock and could sit down to a normal dinner, afterwards watch television or read or go to the movies, and get to bed at a reasonable hour. But what we tell you has nothing to do with what will actually happen. That depends mostly on you, on the kind of person you are. If your life is well-ordered, you probably won't have any trouble. If you tend to delay and wait till the last minute, then each issue of your newspaper is likely to be a harrowing experience, with moments of real suspense when you wonder if you can possibly finish in time. Of course, some people enjoy suspense.

Fortunately, most people seem to be able to adapt to deadline pressure after a while. The secret is not to allow yourself to be upset, but rather to let the force of the approaching deadline suffuse you with inspiration and purpose. If this doesn't happen to you, if you are the kind of person who is always late, then you probably shouldn't get into the newspaper business.

Glossary

agate line, measurement of vertical area roughly equal to 5½ points. Chiefly used in billing display advertising, with 14 agate lines to the inch.

ascender, that portion of a lower-case letter projecting above the mean ine, or x-height. Also, the letter itself with such a projection.

banner, large headline on the front page.

baseline, that on which the bottoms of primary letters align.

blackout, black, red, or orange material pasted onto layout sheet to create a window on the negative into which printer can insert material that has been separately photographed.

blocked ads, those positioned so that they form a rectangle on the page.

blowup, enlargement of illustration or text matter.

boldface, letter of normal form and width but with heavier strokes.

break page, first page of any section beyond the first; also called *section page.*

bulk rate, third-class postage, often used for "junk mail."

byline, that which identifies the writer of an article, usually seen at the beginning but sometimes at the end.

camera-ready, any copy in finished form, ready for the printer to photograph. Used frequently in reference to advertisements supplied by the client that have no need of further typesetting or layout work.

caption, explanatory matter accompanying illustration; also called *cutline.*

classified ad, advertising set in body type with little or no display type, and grouped by subjects. Also called *want ad* or *line ad.*

cold type, type matter not set by means of movable metal type, that is, produced by photographic or strike-on methods of typography.

column inch, area one inch deep and one column wide; used for measuring newspaper contents, especially advertising.

compact format, newspaper format approximately half the size of standard newspaper page, usually 14 to 17 inches deep and with a more conservative makeup than tabloid page using same size sheet.

composition, the setting and arranging of type.

continuous tone, photographic or other art in which gradations of grey or hues are present.

controlled circulation, special second-class postage rate for free-distribution newspapers.

co-op advertising, ads cooperatively paid for by a local merchant and a national sponsor of some product.

copy, all original material to be converted to type, especially news matter.

copy edit, to correct written material for errors in style, grammar, content, and so forth.

copy fit, to determine mathematically the area a given amount of copy will occupy as type.

copyright, legal right to exclusive publication, sale, production, or distribution of a literary, artistic, musical, or dramatic work.

credit line, that which identifies person who has made photograph or artwork appearing in newspaper.

crop-marks, indications of the margins surrounding photographic material or artwork, showing which portions of the material are to be used.

cutline, explanatory material accompanying illustration; caption.

cutoff rule, thin, horizontal dividing line in newspaper page.

dateline, words at opening of news story showing origin and date of filing. Incorrectly used for *folio lines* (which see).

descender, that portion of a lower-case letter projecting below the baseline. Also, the letter itself with such a projection.

display ad, advertising that uses larger than body type and is set off from the text of the newspaper by rules, white space, or decorative devices.

display type, that which is arranged to be conspicuous or appealing to the eye; usually larger than body or text type.

double truck, advertisement on center spread of newspaper, designed to make use of gutters between pages.

dummy, a drawn plan of the layout of the newspaper page, for use in preparing final material.

editorial, article of comment representing the newspaper's opinion. Also, all matter in the newspaper that is not advertising.

em, blank space in a square the size of the type. Not to be confused with pica space.

en, vertical half of em space.

face, style or cut of type.

feature, written material in a newspaper of a nature other than news.

filler, miscellaneous short news items, items of interest, or public service advertisements, used to fill up spaces in newspaper page layout.

flag, name of newspaper in display form on front page; also called *nameplate*. Incorrectly called masthead.

flat, white layout sheet onto which newspaper copy is pasted.

flush left, type set so lines align at left margin.

flush right, type set so lines align at right margin.

folio lines, page numbers, dates, and name of newspaper set in small type at head or foot of newspaper pages.

font, collection of type characters necessary for setting copy in one size and one face.

freelance, a person, especially a writer or artist, who sells services without requiring a long-term commitment to employment.

glossy print, a photograph printed on shiny paper, the preferred kind for newspaper reproduction.

gutter, margins between facing pages.

hairline, thinnest rule used in newspapers.

halftone, continuous tone copy reproduced by means of photographing the image through a screen, breaking it up into a pattern of dots or lines that can then be printed. Halftone screens for offset-printed newspapers usually contain 85 lines to the inch.

headline, display type placed over body type and serving as title for the material below.

hot type, traditional composition method using metal, in contrast to photographic or strike-on type composition; in newspapers, usually linotype.

house ad, advertisement inserted by a newspaper as a promotional device for itself.

indicia, legal data indicating newspaper's qualifications for second-class mailing permit.

insert, separately printed material or newspaper section that must be inserted, usually manually, into the regular edition.

italic, form of typeface that slants to the right.

jump, to continue story from one page in a newspaper to another.

justified copy, type set so that left and right margins are straight.

knockout, black, red, or orange material pasted onto layout sheet to create a window in the negative. See *blackout.*

layout sheet, backing sheet, printed with guiding rules in nonreproducible ink, used as base for copy to be pasted up in form of newspaper page.

leader, ("leeder"), row of dots or dashes connecting two or more elements in a table.

leading, ("ledding"), spacing between lines of type.

legal notice, a paid legal advertisement.

letterpress, printing in which a raised image captures ink and deposits it on paper.

letter-spacing, additional spacing between letters in a typeset word.

libel, any written or printed statement that damages a living person by defamation or ridicule.

light table, table with glass top, constructed so that light from below shines through glass; useful in aligning material on printed sheets.

line art, artwork that appears in simple masses of black and white, as opposed to continuous tone.

linotype, keyboarded typesetting machine that casts type into solid lines of lead with raised letters.

local, a brief social note or news item, usually of personal interest.

lower-case, small letters of the alphabet.

masthead, collection of information usually found on editorial page, including name of publisher, time and place of publication, and other basic facts of publication. Incorrectly used to refer to *nameplate* (which see).

metro format, the standard size of large newspapers, roughly twice that of compact or tabloid format.

nameplate, name of the newspaper in display form as it appears on front page; also called *flag.* Incorrectly called *masthead* (which see).

newsprint, unbleached paper made from ground wood, used to print newspapers.

offset lithography, printing process in which image is transferred from printing plate to rubber blanket, then offset to paper.

opaque, to remove from negative unwanted marks such as specks of dust, shadows of pasted-on material, and so forth.

op-ed, opposite editorial, page of comment facing editorial page.

pasteup, the process of arranging and affixing to a mechanical pieces of cold type composition in preparation for printing.

photo offset, the process of offset lithography (which see).

photostat, positive image made by photocopying machine; also called *stat.*

phototypesetting, method of type composition in which images are placed photographically on film or paper.

pica, unit of printer's measurement, approximately one-sixth of an inch.

plate, thin metal sheet that is photochemically engraved with image to be printed and then attached to offset press.

point, printer's unit of measurement, approximately 1/72 (.01384) inch.

press release, copy submitted to newspaper as a means of self-promotion by group or individual seeking publicity.

proofread, to read typeset copy for errors in spelling, grammar, and typography.

proportional scale, a circular slide rule used in figuring percentages of enlargement and reduction.

proportional spacing, the allotting of different widths to different characters on a typewriter or typesetting machine.

puff piece, an article whose only purpose is to promote or compliment its subject, often an advertiser.

pyramid, the pattern for arranging advertising matter as a triangle on facing pages.

ragged left, type arranged so that the left margin is not aligned.

ragged right, unjustified type, arranged so that the right margin is not aligned.

reading diagonal, broadly defined path of the reader's eye from top left to lower right on the page.

reverse, printed area with black background on which type appears in white.

roman, perpendicular form of type that is characterized by thinning and swelling of curved strokes and by serifs.

running heads, folio lines at top of page, indicating page numbers, date, name of publication.

sans serif, type style which lacks small finishing strokes at the end of main strokes of each letter.

screen, device used to convert continuous tone art to halftone by means of breaking it into dots of black or white.

serif, small finishing stroke at the end of main stroke of a type letter.

sheetfed press, press that prints on separate rectangular sheets of paper.

sizing, calculating the percentage of enlargement or reduction necessary to fit copy or art into the space allotted to it.

solid set copy, type set without additional interlinear spacing.

stabilization processor, machine used for developing exposed paper produced in phototypesetting.

standing matter, type or art that remains in the newspaper each issue without change.

stat, photostatic copy.

strike-on, composition method where image is produced by direct contact between type face and paper, as in typewriting.

subhead, short line of centered text type, usually in bold face, used to break up long columns of body type.

tabloid, newspaper format with page size approximately 11 by 15 inches, or half the size of the standard large newspaper page. Often used to refer to small-format newspapers with very bold, brash design. See *compact format*.

tear sheet, a page torn out of the printed newspaper, usually used as proof to an advertiser that his ad has appeared.

tombstone, headlines placed side by side.

transfer lettering, type lettering which can be transferred from a master sheet to paper by rubbing.

T-square, instrument used with a straight edge to align graphic material on the page.

typeface, any one of the various forms of a type style (which see), having a particular thickness, width, and angle.

type style, a family of typefaces having a particular design, designated by names such as Bodoni, Century, Futura, and so on.

typo, error made in typesetting.

upper-case, capital letters of the alphabet.

velox, photoprint with image in halftone dot pattern rather than in continuous tones.

volume, all issues of a newspaper published within one year. Number of volume indicates newspaper's age.

wax, material heated and used in affixing cold type matter to paper.

web press, rotary printing press using paper fed from wide rolls of newsprint winding through its machinery.

well, deep, narrow opening for editorial matter between two steep columns of ads.

widow, type line shorter than full line length, especially when it appears at the top of a column or page.

width card or *width plug*, plug-in component of phototypesetting machine, enabling it to compensate for variations in widths of letters from one type style to another.

window, clear area on negative produced by blackout; used by printer to strip in halftone material or other matter separately photographed.

x-height, distance between baseline and mean line of type.

Annotated Bibliography

Arnold, Edmund. *Designing the Total Newspaper.* New York: Harper and Row, 1981. $25.00. A new book by one of the nation's foremost experts on newspaper design.

Brigham, Nancy. *How to Do Leaflets, Newsletters, and Newspapers.* New York: Hastings House, 1982. $7.95. A short booklet crammed with detailed illustrations of how to put together a small publication.

Burke, Clifford. *Printing It.* Berkeley, Calif.: Wingbow Press, 1974. $4.95. A brief handbook that clearly sets forth the principles and methods of offset printing. Lively, readable, and certainly applicable to the beginning newspaper publisher's concerns.

Follett, Wilson. *Modern American Usage.* New York: Hill and Wang, 1966. $12.95 (paper $6.95; a $2.50 mass-market paperback edition is also available from Warner Books). A solid reference work for those who are invariably drawn into disputes about matters of accurate usage.

Garst, Robert E., and Bernstein, Theodore M. *Headlines and Deadlines: A Manual for Copy Editors.* 4th ed. New York: Columbia University Press, 1981. $20.00 (paper $7.50). The best source of advice for headline writing, this readable book by two editors of the New York Times also contains useful material on copy editing.

Hough, Henry Beetle. *Country Editor.* Riverside, Conn.: Chatham Press, 1974. $3.95. Probably the best book ever written about small-town journalism. It was originally published in 1940, when Henry and Elizabeth Hough had already been editing and publishing the Vineyard Gazette, on the island of

Martha's Vineyard, for twenty years. Mrs. Hough died in 1965; but her husband continues as editor to this day, though the Gazette has since been sold to James and Sally Reston.

_____ . *Once More the Thunderer.* New York: Ives Washburn, 1950. (Out of print.) Further adventures of the country editor, and further inspiration and consolation for the rest of us.

Kennedy, Bruce M. *Community Journalism: A Way of Life.* Ames, Iowa: Iowa State University Press, 1974. $11.95. Geared to the older style of small-town newspaper—one with a backshop filled with Linotype machines and job presses—this book nevertheless contains much useful information. Its chapter on advertising is outstanding; and it has much to say about the relationship between editor and community.

McKinney, John. *How to Start Your Own Community Newspaper.* Port Jefferson, N.Y.: Meadow Press, 1977. $19.95. Though this book is disorganized and somewhat sloppy, the chapters on business management are interesting.

Newsom, D. Earl, et al. *The Newspaper: Everything You Need to Know to Make It in the Newspaper Business.* Englewood Cliffs, N.J.: Prentice-Hall, 1981. Twenty-eight assorted essays by twenty-eight "media experts," with varying levels of interest to the small independent newspaper publisher. This volume could serve as an excellent text for a course in ugly and confusing book design. The chapter on news writing is quite good, though.

Phillips, Michael, and Rasberry, Salli. *Honest Business: A Superior Strategy for Starting and Managing Your Own Business.* New York: Random House, 1981. $6.00. Provides pointers both practical and philosophical about running a small enterprise.

Strunk, William, Jr., and White, E. B. *The Elements of Style.* 3rd ed. New York: Macmillan, 1979. $2.95. This very short book manages to explain, in a series of rules and admonitions, the virtually unexplainable: how to write well. Absolutely essential for writers and editors.

University of Chicago Press. *The Chicago Manual of Style.* 13th ed. Chicago: University of Chicago Press, 1982. $25.00. The editor's and typographer's most complete and established source on all matters of usage—punctuation, capitalization, abbreviations, hyphenation, distinctive treatment of words, and so on.

Van Uchelen, Rod. *Pasteup: Art Production for the New Art World.* New York: Van Nostrand Reinhold, 1976. $14.95 (paper $7.95). A comprehensive manual dealing with all aspects of pasteup.

Watkins, Don. *The Newspaper Advertising Handbook.* Columbia, S.C.: Newspaper Book Service (P.O. Box 50342). $7.95.

Willis, F. H. *Fundamentals of Layout.* New York: Dover, 1971. $3.50. This book is geared for slick magazines more than for small newspapers. If you're starting a magazine, it's worth reading.

Zinsser, William K. *On Writing Well: An Informal Guide to Writing Nonfiction.* 2nd ed. New York: Harper and Row, 1980. $11.50. One of the best books on writing; the way it is written alone speaks volumes about how to write clearly and directly. Zinsser is an experienced journalist.

PERIODICALS

Columbia Journalism Review, 700 Journalism Building, Columbia University, New York, N.Y. 10027. $16.00 per year. This self-styled "media watchdog" magazine concentrates on big-city and broadcast journalism, but is useful and entertaining reading for all editors. Its back-page feature, "The Lower Case," is itself worth the price of a subscription.

Editor and Publisher, 850 Third Avenue, New York, N.Y. 10022. $15.00 per year. Somewhat stodgy but often helpful, this weekly magazine carries ads for used equipment and newspapers for sale all over the country. Good browsing.

Glitches: Compugraphic Users' Newsletter. Drawer 5007, Bend, Ore. 97708. $25.00 for ten issues. A monthly compendium of shared advice, warnings, and sources of Compugraphic typesetting equipment and repairs. Essential as the industry changes in favor of high-priced systems.

The Harvard Post, P.O. Box 308, Harvard, Mass. 01451. $10.00 per year. For the really curious.

TypeWorld, 15 Oakridge Circle, Wilmington, Mass. 01887. $20.00 per year (free to newspaper publishers). The trade newspaper of the typesetting and word processing industry. Lots of corporate press releases, choked with jargon and doublespeak, but also much essential information about new developments in a rapidly changing field.

[*Note:* We've been thinking about starting a newsletter for small newspaper editors and publishers, covering all the topics included in this book and serving as a clearinghouse for sharing ideas, problems, and solutions. If you're interested, write to us at the address above.]

Index